The Burden He Carried

By

Thomas Smith Jr.

A Memoir

The Burden He Carried

© 2025 Thomas Smith Jr.

All rights reserved.

This is a work of nonfiction. Some names and identifying details have been changed to protect the privacy of individuals.

Printed in the United States of America.

First Edition

ISBN: 9798286055333

Imprint: Independently published

For permissions or inquiries, contact:

Thomas Smith Jr.

Epigraph

"Some burdens aren't passed down.
They aren't told at the dinner table or written in
letters.
Steady hands and quiet eyes are where they live.
They are the weight one man carries alone—
not to protect the truth,
but to protect those he loves from the cost of
knowing it."

Introduction

There are stories that define a generation—tales of war, survival, sacrifice, or progress. But there are other stories—quieter ones—that sit just beneath the surface of history. They're not taught in schools. They're not headlined in textbooks. Yet they carry just as much weight. Sometimes more.

This is one of those stories.

The Burden He Carried is not a tale of fame or fortune. It's not about someone who sought the spotlight or claimed a legacy. This is the story of my father, Thomas Franklin Smith—a quiet, hardworking man born into poverty and segregation in Mississippi, raised in a world built on rules that broke spirits and silenced truth. He was not a politician, a soldier of legend, or a civil rights leader. He was simply a man who lived through it all. And, in the end, he chose to stand.

This book is about what he saw, what he endured, and what

he finally did. He grew up in the Deep South during the Great Depression, where racial lines were drawn not just by law, but by fear and blood.

As a young white boy, he broke one of the most dangerous rules of that time: he formed a secret friendship with a black boy named Jeremiah. Their bond was forged by trust, adventure, and shared dreams—until hatred tore it apart in the most violent way possible. My father witnessed the brutal cost of injustice and lived the rest of his life with the weight of what he couldn't stop.

He went on to serve his country in World War II, witnessing another kind of horror. He returned home, tried to build a life and a family, but the past never loosened its grip. Years later, when his son James faced his own struggles and dangers, he came back. This time, when hate rose again in a new form, he didn't run. He didn't stay silent. He took a stand.

And it changed everything.

The Burden He Carried is about that moment. But more than that, it's about the long road that led to it.

It's a story rooted in the American South—in red dirt roads, cotton fields, small-town fear, and the kind of quiet strength born out of survival. It's about the inheritance of silence, the legacy of trauma, and the deeply human desire to protect those we love, even when the system refuses to protect us.

It is also a deeply personal book. My father never asked me to write it. He didn't tell me to share these truths. But in the final years of his life, as we spent time together—working on the land, sitting in quiet conversation—I came to understand that there were stories he was finally ready to let go of. And I knew someone had to carry them.

This book is for readers who want to see the human face of American history. For those who believe the personal and political are always connected. For anyone who has ever felt the weight of injustice—whether they were its target, its witness, or someone trying to make sense of it all. It's for people who know that sometimes, the hardest part of truth isn't speaking it—it's living with it.

So, this is my offering:

A story passed from father to son.

A history lived, not imagined.

And a quiet man, who stood tall when it mattered most.

Now that story is yours.

— *Thomas Smith Jr.*

Table of Contents

,

.

Thomas Smith Jr. is an aspiring author whose life experiences and quiet observations have finally found their voice in print. His debut novel, 'The Burden He Carried,' reflects years of thought, memory, and truth passed down through generations. With more stories in the works, Thomas continues to write with a deep sense of purpose, sharing personal and historical legacies that explore family, struggle, and resilience. He writes not only to remember, but to bear witness - and to honor those who came before.

Chapter 1

Mississippi

Low in the Mississippi sky, the sun cast long shadows across the seemingly endless cotton fields. It was the 1930s, and Mississippi, like much of the Southern United States, was grappling with the harsh realities of a struggling agrarian economy, exacerbated by the grip of the Great Depression. The air was thick with the smell of sweat and soil, a reminder of the endless toil that defined life in the rural South. For the men and women who worked the fields—most of them sharecroppers—each day was a battle, not just with the land, but with the system that kept them tethered to it.

The system's inherent racism made life even harder for African American sharecroppers. In Mississippi, discrimination was part of everyday life. Often, lenders denied black farmers fair loans, good market prices, and access to supplies. Landowners forced many to sign unfair contracts that gave them all the power. Even though slavery had ended after the Civil War, a new control took its place— one based on poverty and racism that kept black families trapped in a life of struggle.

The daily grind of a sharecropper's life was unforgiving. Days began well before dawn, with families rising to the crow of roosters, readying themselves for another grueling day in the fields. The Mississippi heat, oppressive and unyielding, bore down on them as they bent low to tend to the cotton, their hands raw from pulling the prickly bolls from the plants. For many families, parents sent children as young as five or six years old into the fields to work alongside them. The whole family's survival depended on their combined effort.

Men, women, and children worked long days under the hot Mississippi sun. The work never seemed to end, and their success depended on things they couldn't control—like the weather, insects, and crop prices. One poor season could ruin everything. If the crops failed, debts piled up fast, and landowners still expected to be paid. Families worried constantly, watching dark clouds roll in or spotting signs of bugs in the fields, knowing that just one storm or a swarm of pests could wipe out months of hard labor.

Mornings began with hope, but by afternoon, the sun's

punishing rays would sap the energy from their bodies, leaving them drenched in sweat, their muscles aching, and their spirits flagging. They labored for long hours, often working from sunup to sundown. They cherished the brief moments of respite—a sip of water, a bite of cornbread—but these moments were short-lived.

At night, after a full day in the fields, sharecropping families would return to their homes—ramshackle cabins provided by the landowners. These homes were little more than drafty, single-room shacks with leaky roofs and dirt floors. They offered scant protection from the elements, the summer heat searing through thin wooden walls, and the winter cold creeping in through every crack. There was no electricity, no plumbing, no luxuries. At night, families huddled together, their bodies aching from the day's labor, praying for better weather, a better crop, a better tomorrow.

Inside these homes, everything was barebones—mattresses stuffed with straw, a stove for cooking, and maybe a single chair. With the little money they had left after paying off debts to the landowner, most families could barely afford food, let alone furnishings. Meals were often meager, comprising beans, bread, and whatever vegetables they could grow in their small garden patches. Meat was a rare treat. The constant threat of hunger hovered over these families, a reminder of just how fragile their existence was.

Sharecropping was a hard and unfair way to live. Families worked all day, every day, but still couldn't get ahead. If their crops didn't grow well, they owed even more money to the landowner. Their debt kept getting bigger every year. When the Great Depression began, things got worse. Cotton wasn't worth much anymore, so farmers made very little money. Some landowners, who also had a hard time, sold their land or raised the rent. That made it even harder for sharecroppers who needed the land just to feed their families and survive.

Each year, the landowners forced sharecroppers to settle accounts. After selling the cotton crop, the landowner would deduct the costs of seed, fertilizer, tools, and rent. For many, it was a cruel surprise when the reckoning came. Despite working dawn to dusk, they often found themselves deeper in debt than they had been at the start of the year. Some years, they made little more than pennies for months of labor.

Landowners almost always wrote the contracts to benefit

themselves, leaving sharecroppers with no actual way to fight back. Landowners controlled everything—the prices, the markets, and the rules. They often charged extremely high prices for seeds, tools, and other supplies, making it nearly impossible for sharecroppers to get out of debt. If a sharecropper couldn't pay what they owed, the landowner would make them stay and work another year. This cycle kept families stuck in poverty. Many dreamed of owning their own land and building a better life, but those dreams slowly faded with each passing year.

Debt trapped families on the land, year after year, with no way out. The children of sharecroppers grew up expecting the same hard life—long days of exhausting work and the same deep poverty their parents faced, with little chance for a better future.

Life was even harder for African American sharecroppers because of segregation and Jim Crow laws. These rules weren't just written—they affected everyday life. Signs that said "Whites Only" were placed outside stores, restaurants, and schools. Black people had separate places to go, but they were often old, dirty, or broken. The unfair treatment was everywhere. They had to use poor restrooms, drink from

"Colored Only" water fountains, and even step off the sidewalk to let white people pass.

The omnipresent threat of violence hung over every interaction. Scorn, violence, arrest, or lynching could befall a black man who failed to step off the sidewalk for a white person. The Ku Klux Klan, ever present in the Deep South, was a force of terror. African Americans lived in constant fear of being falsely accused of a crime or slight, knowing that the punishment could be a public execution.

Lynchings were a constant danger and created deep fear in black communities. The Ku Klux Klan carried out these violent acts without punishment, and the police often looked the other way—or sometimes even helped. Stories of black people who were killed or went missing for doing something as simple as speaking out or looking the wrong way spread quickly. These stories reminded everyone to stay quiet and not challenge the rules, or they could be next.

In the 1930s Mississippi, lynching was more than just a terrible crime—it was a tool used to enforce white control and keep black people living in fear. These brutal acts were not hidden; they were carried out in public, often with crowds watching. People sometimes left the bodies of black men, women, and even children hanging from trees for days, serving as a horrifying warning to others. These lynchings sent a clear message: Black lives did not matter, and anyone could lose their freedom at any moment. It was a cruel system meant to keep black families silent, scared, and in their so-called "place."

Segregation touched every part of life, and education was no exception. For black children, going to school was a rare chance, and even then, the conditions were often terrible. Many had to learn in old, falling-apart buildings—small, one-room shacks with broken windows, leaky roofs, and scarcely enough desks or chairs for everyone. These schools had almost no money and very few supplies. They rarely had enough books, pencils, or even chalkboards. There were rarely enough teachers, and the few who taught had to handle large groups of students of all ages and grade levels at the same time.

Attendance was often irregular. Farm work prevented most of the children from attending school regularly. For families living in poverty, every pair of hands counted, and missing a day of work—even for school—meant less food on the table. Education became a luxury, not a guarantee, and many black children grew up without ever finishing a basic grade level. Yet even with all these challenges, families still tried to make sure their children learned what they could, hoping it might lead to a better life one day.

In many rural areas, where there were no proper schools for black children, learning had to happen in secret. A few people from the black community—some self-taught, others with only a little education—would take time to teach the children whenever they could. During fieldwork breaks, these volunteers gathered small groups and taught them basic reading, writing, and math. These makeshift schools were often tucked away in quiet, out-of-sight places, far from the eyes of the landowners. Landowners didn't want black workers to get an education. They believed that if workers became educated, they might start asking for fair treatment—and that would upset the way things were.

Despite the exhaustion that came from working long hours in the fields, children showed an incredible thirst for knowledge. Most black sharecroppers had only a third-grade education. Still, their thirst for knowledge was palpable. Children, despite their exhaustion from long hours of fieldwork, would absorb whatever lessons they could, their minds yearning for more than just survival. They wanted to know about the world beyond the cotton fields and the riverbanks. Even when forced to the margins, their spirits sought freedom through learning.

The economic downturn during the Great Depression didn't just impact the sharecroppers themselves. It ravaged the entire region. Landowners, unable to make payments on taxes or mortgages, lost their holdings. Some fled to the cities, hoping to find industrial work—though for black men, factory jobs were often closed off. Employers preferred white laborers, and black families faced unemployment rates three times higher than white families. Even basic needs like food were out of reach for many black families, as soup kitchens and aid organizations often turned them away, offering their services only to white people.

Black communities in Mississippi stayed strong, even through hard times. They faced hunger, poverty, and unfair treatment every day, but they didn't give up. Families helped each other by sharing food and supplies. Churches were more than places to pray—they gave out food and offered comfort and hope. After long, tiring days in the fields, neighbors would gather to cook and eat together. These simple acts of kindness brought people closer and helped them stay strong through the struggle.

A shared struggle for survival and a deep hope for a better future tightly bound rural black communities. Even under the heavy weight of segregation and poverty, they found ways to celebrate life. Weddings, births, and Sunday gatherings brought moments of joy, where laughter and music offered a break from daily hardship. The sound of blues, gospel, and work songs drifted through the fields and homes—a powerful reminder that while their bodies labored, their spirits remained free.

Still faced with so much hardship, there was hope. Change was taking root—not only in Mississippi, but throughout the South. The strength of black communities, the growing awareness of their suffering, and the early signs of a movement for justice were coming together. Mississippi's sharecroppers, with their tired hands and unshaken spirits, were planting the seeds of something bigger—a fight that would one day challenge the deep roots of segregation and economic injustice.

The struggle of the sharecroppers was not in vain. Though they toiled in obscurity, though the land seemed to claim more from them than it ever gave, their resilience became a cornerstone for the broader civil rights movement that would follow. From the cotton fields of Mississippi to the halls of justice, their fight for dignity, equality, and freedom would ripple through the generations.

Mississippi's fields may have been harsh, its sun relentless, and its laws unjust, but the spirit of those who lived and worked in its soil would prove stronger than the forces that sought to break them.

In the Mississippi countryside, many white families struggled to raise their children during the Great Depression. The cotton economy had fallen apart, leaving small towns filled with worry and hardship. Wealthy landowners and business owners could get by because they had money saved. But most working families, who labored every day just to put food on the table, suffered, having few resources to fall back on.

Among these struggling families was the Smith family, a household of ten, doing their best to survive on the outskirts of Stonewall, Mississippi. The Smiths had eight children, and each played a vital role in the daily upkeep of their modest homestead. The youngest of the Smith's children was Thomas—my father—who, like his siblings, knew no life outside of hard work and responsibility.

The Smiths lived in a modest wooden farmhouse, with a tin roof that echoed with the soft rhythm of rain during storms. Though simple, sturdy hands built the house, and it has withstood the test of time. It sat at the top of a small hill overlooking a stretch of farmland and gravel road that led to the small town of Stonewall. Mulberry trees, blackberry bushes, and honeysuckle lined the property, filling the air with their sweet scents in the spring.

At the back of the house was a large garden, the family's lifeline. The household expected every member to contribute to the garden's upkeep. The family carefully tended rows of corn, beans, squash, and tomatoes, while patches of sweet potatoes and turnips provided additional sustenance. It was a constant battle against pests, poor soil, and unpredictable weather, but there was no other choice. The garden wasn't just a source of food—it was survival.

Thomas, though the youngest, was no exception to the daily workload. From the moment the sun peeked over the horizon, he was outside, feeding the chickens, gathering eggs, or pulling weeds from between the rows of vegetables. His hands, though small, were rough from the constant work. Unlike children in wealthier towns, there was no time for idle play. Labor and necessity shaped his childhood. In between all the chores, he could attend a small school two miles from the family home.

At the heart of the family was Alice Smith, Thomas's mother. A woman of unwavering strength and compassion, Alice bore the weight of raising eight children with grace and resilience. She not only cared for her own family but also served as a midwife for the surrounding community.

The countryside lacked doctors, so expectant mothers relied on experienced women like Alice to deliver their babies. She had learned midwifery from her own mother, passing down knowledge that had sustained generations of families in Mississippi. When a neighbor's time came, day or night, Alice would gather her things—a clean sheet, scissors, cloth for swaddling—and make her way through the fields and dirt roads to help deliver a child into the world.

Her work as a midwife didn't bring in much money, but in a time when families had little to offer, payment often came as fresh eggs, a bag of cornmeal, or whatever else the family could spare. Despite the challenges of raising her own children, she never hesitated to help another mother in need.

She was the backbone of the Smith family, the matriarch who ensured that her children never went hungry, even if it meant going without herself.

While Alice kept the home running, Oscar Smith, Thomas's father, worked to support his family. He had been fortunate to have steady work at one of the cotton mills in Stonewall, a job that provided a much-needed income. The mills were the lifeblood of the town, employing hundreds of men to process and weave cotton.

For years, Oscar woke before dawn and drove the dusty road to the mill, where he spent long hours operating heavy machinery in hot, windowless rooms. The air was thick with cotton dust, coating his clothes and lungs, making it difficult to breathe. The pay wasn't great, but it was enough to put food on the table and keep the family afloat.

However, as the Great Depression worsened, the mill began

cutting back hours. The demand for cotton had plummeted, and one by one, workers found themselves without jobs. At first, Oscar was lucky—the mill reduced his hours, but he still brought home a paycheck. But as the months passed and the economic downturn deepened, the inevitable happened.

One evening, he returned home later than usual, his face drawn with worry. He sat at the wooden kitchen table, staring at his calloused hands as he broke the news to Alice. His employer had laid him off.

For a moment, the room was silent. The younger children were asleep, and the older ones listened from their beds. Alice, ever resilient, took a deep breath and placed her hand on his.

"We'll manage," she whispered.

But even she knew things were about to get harder.

Without the mill income, the Smiths had to rely even more on their garden and the kindness of neighbors. Oscar took whatever odd jobs he could find—chopping wood, fixing roofs, even trapping small game for food. But work was scarce, and many men in Stonewall were in the same situation.

The family tightened their belts. Alice learned to stretch every meal, making soups from whatever scraps she could find. They made cornbread a staple, reserving meat for Sundays or special occasions. Thomas and his siblings scoured the nearby woods for wild berries and nuts, anything to supplement their meager meals.

Oscar refused to let his children go hungry. He spent his evenings hunting rabbits and squirrels, skinning and cleaning them on the back porch before Alice cooked them over the wood stove. When they were lucky, he'd return with a catfish from the river, a rare treat that was always savored.

Despite their struggles, the family found solace in each other. The children, though young, understood the importance of working together. There were no complaints, no protests— only the quiet determination to make it through another day.

Even in hardship, the people of Stonewall came together. The Smiths weren't the only family struggling, and in small towns like theirs, neighbors took care of one another.

Families traded goods when they could—fresh eggs for flour, hand-sewn clothes for firewood. Church gatherings became a place of comfort, a refuge where families could share their burdens and find strength in their faith. The congregation sang hymns of hope on Sundays; their voices soared above the surrounding despair.

Alice's reputation as a midwife earned her the respect and gratitude of the community. Women who had once been in her care often stopped by with small offerings—a jar of preserves, a loaf of bread, a bundle of greens from their garden. These slight gestures of kindness made all the difference.

For the children, joy still found its way into their lives. Thomas and his brothers carved wooden toys from scraps of wood, their imaginations transforming them into horses, wagons, and soldiers. On warm summer evenings, they chased fireflies through the fields, their laughter echoing through the night.

As the years passed, the Great Depression did not loosen its grip. But through the hardship, the Smiths endured. Their story was not one of wealth or privilege but of perseverance, of a family that held on to each other when everything else seemed uncertain.

Oscar never gave up looking for work. As the economy improved, he would finally get a job with the railroad. It brought a steadier income and helped give the family some stability. Alice kept working as a midwife, helping deliver babies in the community, even while she was struggling to feed her own children at home.

For young Thomas, these years shaped him into the man he would become. He learned the value of hard work, the importance of family, and the quiet strength of resilience. He would carry these lessons with him for the rest of his life, passing them down to the next generation.

Though the Smiths never became wealthy, they had something far more valuable—each other. And in a time when survival was uncertain, that was the greatest wealth of all.

As a young white boy, Thomas became friends with a black boy named Jeremiah, who lived on a caretaker farm between my father's family home and the river. Often, they would make loud crow sounds to let each other know when to meet on the trail. My father would call out "craw craw craw" code for I am here, can you come? The other boy would call out two times "craw craw" to reply yes, I am on my way or just one "craw" for no, I can't leave. Thomas and Jeremiah's crow calls were so realistic, they fooled everyone. Sometimes even they would be fooled by an actual crow calling in the forest that they would answer back. My father knew he had to be very cautious, because segregation was very real at the time and it was forbidden for a white and black boy to be together as close friends. The boys felt so strongly about their secret that they both agreed to never tell anyone about it, not even their own families.

Jeremiah's family lived on a farm where the family was involved in the sharecropping system. They lived in an old clapboard house side by side with 4 other houses, all with black families who worked on the farm. Each family would have a good-sized garden and grew most all the food the family needed. The landowner expected these sharecroppers to farm the land in which the major crop was cotton, and at the end of the year, they made a small profit. The outhouses were on the downhill side of the houses and away from the water supply.

Both boys had made crude fishing poles, and they learned how to place trotlines across the width of the river. Each trotline would have up to 5 separate line segments with baited hooks. They would catch fish and cook them over an open campfire on the river's edge and bring some back to share with the family. Thomas and Jeremiah would lie on the riverbank and talk and dream of adventure and what the future may hold for them. The boys vigilantly watched for others near the river, knowing the consequences of white and black boys being caught together. If the boys saw anyone in the distance, they would hide until the danger passed. They continued their friendship during their younger years meeting as often as possible with that "craw craw craw" echoing through the forest as the boys would meet again.

As the boys reached 17 years old, they decided to join the navy and see the world. During the 40s there were very few blacks in the military, only around 2% of the entire force. Jeremiah saw this as his one chance to escape poverty and build a future for himself. It was a very exciting time, as both Thomas and Jeremiah were going to see the world and serve their country at the same time. They made an appointment the following week to go into Jackson Mississippi on Monday morning to sign the papers to enter military service.

On a bright Saturday morning, Thomas walked down the trail towards Jeremiah's house and called out, "craw craw craw", no answer came back from Jeremiah. Thomas sat on the trail for an hour and tried the crow call again, "craw craw craw", still no answer from Jeremiah. Finding it unusual that Jeremiah didn't return his call, Thomas went down the path to the river to fish alone. After a couple of hours, Thomas gave up fishing and walked to the nearby town of Stonewall to visit the general store to get a soda.

As Thomas neared the eastern edge of town, he spotted five buzzards circling low over a wooded hill. Curious and uneasy, he followed the direction of their flight, weaving through the trees in silence. He moved carefully, each step heavier than the last. Then he heard voices—angry, shouting, cruel—and froze behind a thick oak tree. Through the branches, he saw a group of white-robed men gathered beneath a large tree. Thomas's heart pounded as he realized what was happening. The Ku Klux Klan had Jeremiah!

Powerless and terrified, Thomas stayed hidden, barely breathing, as the men dragged his friend beneath the tree. He watched in horror as they slipped a noose around Jeremiah's neck. With one brutal motion, they threw the rope over a branch and lifted him from the ground. Thomas wanted to scream, to run, to do anything—but his legs wouldn't move. All he could do was watch.

When the men finally disappeared into the woods, laughing and triumphant, Thomas crawled from his hiding place. He fell to his knees beneath the tree, weeping. Jeremiah's body hung lifeless above him. Blood-red letters on a note pinned to his shirt read: "ONE MORE NIGGER DEAD."

In a panic, Thomas ran into town to the sheriff's office to report the lynching of his friend Jeremiah. He told the sheriff he found a black boy hanging in the woods nearby but was very careful not to say he knew him or that they were friends. The sheriff wrote a few notes and told Thomas to just go home and forget about what he had just found, and he would take care of the problem. To this sheriff in this small Mississippi town, the lynching of a black was the same importance as writing a speeding ticket and not investigated any further. The sheriff sent out two deputies to cut the rope and just let the body slam to the ground. They brought the body to the local morgue and would only give a couple days for anyone to claim the body before they put would put it into an unmarked grave in the blacks-only cemetery.

Heartbroken, Thomas started his walk back home along the dirt trail winding through the hills. As he came to the place just below Jeremiah's house, he stopped, put his hands to his face, and cried in grief for his lost friend. At that moment, he decided to walk to Jeremiah's house and tell them the news of Jeremiah's death. An older woman in a cooking apron stood on the front porch as he approached and asked, "what do y'all want here boy?" Thomas asked if she was Jeremiah's mother, and she replied that she was.

Thomas broke down crying again as he told Jeremiah's mother of how he found him hanging from the tree near town. The mother fell to her knees, crying as the rest of Jeremiah's family came out and heard the devastating news of Jeremiah's death. Again and again, the black community continued to struggle with another tragedy, but this time, it hit close to home.

Jeremiah's father jumped into the farm's only pickup truck and drove into Jackson to pick up Jeremiah's body from the morgue.

Thomas returned home and gathered the strength to tell his

mother and father the horrific news of his friend's death. That weekend was the worst time of Thomas's life as he tried to sort out what he should do. He hated how people of color were treated in Mississippi; it broke his heart. He would never forget his friend Jeremiah for the rest of his life. As Monday came around, Thomas went to the Jackson navy recruitment center and signed the paperwork to enter the navy.

Chapter 2

Navy Service

Thomas stood on the banks of the river one last time, the thick summer air clinging to his skin like a second layer of sweat and memory. The humidity curled the edges of his hair and soaked through the back of his shirt, but he scarcely noticed. He had walked this path a thousand times before— down from the back of the old church, through the wildflower thickets, and across the muddy clearing where the cypress roots knuckled up from the soil like bones. His feet knew every dip, every hidden stone, the soft give of the Mississippi mud underfoot. But today, everything felt different. The familiar no longer comforted him—it pressed in around him, heavy and reluctant to let go.

The river was restless. It swelled from the banks like something alive and angry, swollen by last night's relentless rain. The brown current had turned darker, churned to a muddy, opaque chocolate that masked its depth. Bits of driftwood, leaves, and broken branches spun in lazy eddies before being sucked downstream. It moved with purpose, as if the water itself was in a hurry to leave, to get far away from this quiet stretch of Southern land and everything that came with it. Just like him.

Thomas stood still, watching the river pull the world apart piece by piece. He wondered if anyone else in this town ever stopped to watch it like this. Did they see the way the water cut through the land, the way it eroded without apology? Or had they grown numb to it, the way they had grown numb to everything else that had faded from what it once was?

He crouched and scooped a fistful of the red Mississippi clay, the soil cool and slick against his calloused palm. It oozed between his fingers as he held it tight for a moment before letting it slip back to the earth. It stained his skin a rusty hue, stubborn and deep. Just like the memories that clung to him, no matter how far he went. This place had marked him, shaped him in ways he didn't thoroughly understand. And now it was asking him to let it go.

A soft breeze stirred the trees overhead, rustling their branches like whispers. Cicadas droned in a hypnotic rhythm, and a lone bird cried out from the other side of the water, its call thin and mournful. These were the sounds of home— sounds that once lulled him to sleep in the dead heat of July, that filled the silence on long walks when no one else would come with him. He had etched these sounds into his bones, but now they felt foreign, as if he were already elsewhere.

He closed his eyes and let the wind move over him, trying to commit it all to memory: the feel of the air, the smell of river mud and honeysuckle, the dull roar of the water against the stones. He didn't know when he'd return, or if he ever would. Leaving wasn't a decision—it was a necessity. But it felt like betrayal.

He opened his eyes and looked out over the river one last time. Then he turned and walked back up the path, each step pulling him further from the only life he'd ever known.

His thoughts drifted back—unwilling, but unstoppable—to his boyhood days along this river, to the hours he'd spent beneath the summer sun with Jeremiah. Back then, the world had felt wide open, like anything was possible. They'd fish for hours in silence or chatter about everything and nothing at all, the lines of race and poverty blurred by the muddy waters of the Mississippi. A white boy and a black boy, barefoot and grinning, thick as thieves. In those moments, out there with the wind and the water, they were just kids. Equals. Free.

But the world beyond the trees didn't see it that way. It never had.

They'd dreamed big, the way boys do—talked about joining the Navy together, seeing the Pacific, the Mediterranean, places neither of them could spell but both could picture. They'd lie on their backs in the grass and map out their futures like a pair of sailors plotting a course. Thomas had believed it. Every word, for a time, Jeremiah had too.

But that time was gone. And so was Jeremiah.

Thomas's jaw clenched as he remembered that day—how the air had gone still and sour before he even reached the grove. He hadn't meant to find him. He was just walking, thinking, the way he always did when things got heavy. But something had pulled him off the path that morning, something deep in his gut. And then there he was— Jeremiah!

Hanging from a low branch like some ragged scarecrow, his shirt torn open, his skin marked by rage and rope and fire. The tree had groaned in the wind, its limbs swaying like it had been asked to carry a burden it never wanted. The Klan

28

hadn't even bothered to hide him. That was the message—they *wanted* him to be found. They wanted folks to see what happened when a black boy forgot his place.

Thomas hadn't screamed. He couldn't. He had just stood there, shaking, as the cicadas droned on like nothing had changed.

But everything had.

He hadn't spoken of it to anyone—not really. Jeremiah's mother had already known, in the way mothers do. She'd looked at Thomas like she could see the image burned into the backs of his eyes. And the town… the town had gone on, like it always did. Like Jeremiah had never existed. Like Thomas hadn't stood in the shadow of a murder and walked away with his soul cracked in two.

It was the Depression. Folks were hungry. Angry. Looking for someone to blame. And in a place like this, men with white hoods didn't need excuses—they just needed permission. And silence was permission enough.

Thomas had never forgiven himself for being part of that

silence. Not really. He hadn't spoken out. Hadn't named names. What could a white boy do, they'd have said, against the weight of all that hate? But that question would gnaw at him for the rest of his life. What *should* he have done?

Now, as he stood by the river one last time, the ghosts of that day came back stronger than ever. The sound of Jeremiah's laughter filled the air. Jeremiah's dreams. Jeremiah's voice whispering to him in the hush between cicada calls: *"You still breathing, Tommy. That means you still got a chance to do something."*

Maybe that's why Thomas had come here before leaving. Not to say goodbye—but to reckon with the boy he used to be, and the friend he'd lost. Maybe leaving this place wasn't running away. Maybe it was following the path he and Jeremiah had dreamed of—one of oceans and freedom, of escape and purpose. A way to carry Jeremiah forward when the rest of the world had buried him and moved on.

He reached into his pocket and pulled out the dog tag he'd had made for Jeremiah—just a piece of metal, scuffed and worn, but precious. He held it tight, so tight the edges bit into his skin.

"I'm going, Jer," he said softly, his voice thick. "Not because I want to leave. But because I have to. For both of us."

Then he tucked the tag away and continued to walk from the river. The trees behind him rustled, and for just a second, he thought he heard laughter in the wind.

But when he looked back, the river was quiet once more.

The Navy had been an idea that had lingered in the back of Thomas's mind like a low hum ever since the war began. At first, it had been more fantasy than a plan—something he spoke about when the weight of the world felt too heavy, when the town felt too small, or when he needed to believe there was something out there waiting for him. But as the headlines grew grimmer, and more names from nearby towns appeared in the obituaries, that fantasy had hardened something more real. Concrete. Inevitable.

Thomas never backed down from what was expected. Duty wasn't just a word—his family passed it down like a family heirloom. His father, a veteran of the Great War, talked little about the past, but the way he stood, the quiet way he carried pain in his shoulders, told Thomas everything he needed to

31

know. And now, once again, the world was burning. Hitler had taken Poland. London was under siege. The Pacific had gone red. Young men—boys—were being pulled from farms and classrooms and sent to the front lines. And Thomas, with the strength of youth and grief beneath his ribs, knew his time was coming.

But it wasn't *just* the war that stirred something in him. Part of him—maybe a bigger part than he liked to admit— was aching for escape. He didn't hate his hometown. Not exactly. But it had become a place that felt frozen in time, bound up in silence and sorrow. The fields were the same. Church bells rang the same hymns. Townsfolk spoke with the same clipped tones, offered the same tired smiles. The river still carved its slow, stubborn path through the land, as if unaware that the rest of the world was moving on without them.

Thomas needed more than what Mississippi could offer. He wanted more than fields of cotton and dusty roads that led nowhere. He craved something bigger—something that didn't feel like a memory pressing down on his chest. He dreamed of salt in his hair, the steady rise and fall of a ship beneath him, and the endless ocean stretching out like hope.

He longed to be part of something greater than himself—something that could give purpose to the weight he carried.

And though he wouldn't admit it—not even to himself—the Navy also offered him a way to leave Jeremiah's ghost behind.

But standing here now, on the riverbank that had once been their world, that decision no longer felt so simple. The weight of what he was about to do settled on him like the humidity—slow, oppressive, hard to shake. The idea of war felt more than noble or necessary. It felt terrifying. Final. The boyish dreams of adventure had given way to the reality of blood, fear, and loss. And even though he had told everyone—his family, the recruiter, even the pastor—that he was ready to serve, in this quiet moment, he wasn't so sure.

For a fleeting second, he considered turning back. He imagined himself walking away from the river, from the Navy, from the unknown. He could stay. Keep working odd jobs. Help his father repair the roof before the next rain. Pretend, for a while longer, that everything was fine.

But deep down, he knew that wasn't an option. The family would drive him to Jackson tomorrow morning. His bags were already packed. That afternoon, his mother had fried chicken, fighting back tears as she worked. His father had clapped a firm hand on Thomas's shoulder that said everything he couldn't.

With a quiet exhale, Thomas rose from the riverbank and wiped his clay-streaked hands on the thighs of his pants, smearing rust-colored stains into the worn fabric. He turned to go, but his eyes caught something in the distance—the faint silhouette of Jeremiah's family home, half-hidden behind the trees.

The old house stood as it had the day Thomas had first walked past it after the funeral. The whitewashed boards had faded to gray in places, but the porch still held its quiet dignity. There were flowers by the front steps—always flowers. Miss Loretta, Jeremiah's mother, kept that house with a quiet pride that defied the hatred that had tried to erase her son. The whole place felt like a memorial now— unchanging, sacred. A house too full of silence and too heavy with the weight of all the things left unsaid.

Thomas stared at it for a long moment, the familiar ache rising in his chest. He had thought, more than once, about stopping by. About telling Miss Loretta that he still thought of Jeremiah every single day. That he carried her boy with him everywhere. But he knew—knew in his bones—that a visit from a white boy like him, especially now, could bring more pain than comfort. The white landowners still watched every move made by the black families that lived on their property, and suspicion came as easy as breathing. The wrong conversation could bring the wrong kind of attention.

Still, the guilt gnawed at him.

Jeremiah had been his best friend. His brother in every way but blood. He'd had a way of making the world feel lighter. Of saying just the right thing to cut through the weight. Thomas could almost hear him now, that soft drawl, that teasing tone.

"Don't get all teary-eyed on me, Tommy. You go do what we talked about. You go and see that damn world."

Maybe Jeremiah would laugh, slap him on the back like he always used to, and tell him to go make them both proud.

35

Thomas swallowed hard and turned away. The trees whispered around him as he walked, their leaves rustling like voices too tired to speak. Each step down the dusty path toward his family's home felt heavier than the last. The sound of the cicadas rose in waves behind him, a steady hum that chased him forward.

This was it. There would be no turning back now.

He was leaving Mississippi.

He was leaving Jeremiah.

But he carried him still.

It will always be so.

When Thomas reached the house, the screen door creaked open before he could touch the handle. His mother stood there on the porch, hands clenched in her apron, her eyes searching his face like she was trying to memorize it. The soft hum of cicadas filled the warm evening air. But all he could hear was the rustle of her apron as she wiped flour from her fingers, over and over, a nervous rhythm that betrayed what her face tried to hide.

The smell of fried chicken drifted out from the kitchen, warm and rich, mingling with the buttery, sweet aroma of fresh cornbread cooling on the windowsill. It hit Thomas like a wave—home. Memory. A part of him wanted to bottle the smell, to carry it with him wherever he went. His mother had been cooking all day; he knew it without her saying so. It was her way of holding him, of keeping him close without the ache of words. Her love was in the way she prepared his plate, in the extra hush puppies she tucked into the basket, in the way she fussed over the tablecloth being straight.

Inside, his father sat in his worn chair by the hearth, the newspaper open but scarcely read. The pages rustled every so often, but Thomas could feel his eyes flicking up over the top of the print, watching him with that quiet intensity that said everything he wouldn't speak aloud. His father had always been a man of action, not emotion—he taught lessons with a firm hand and a steady presence—but even now, he couldn't quite hide the tightness in his jaw, the heaviness in his gaze.

In the kitchen, his older sisters were moving, setting the table with practiced hands, their voices dancing between cheer and caution. They were trying, bless them, to keep the mood light. Joking about burnt biscuits and who was hogging the butter knife. But the laughter never quite reached their eyes. They darted glances toward Thomas when they thought he wasn't looking, as if trying to etch him into their memories, too.

Thomas's brothers came in from the back garden, washed their hands in the utility sink, and sat down at the table. Silent, nervous, but proud of what Thomas planned to do to serve his country.

Everyone knew what tomorrow meant. It hung in the air like a coming storm. Tomorrow, Thomas would be gone—off to Jackson, off to boot camp, off to a war none of them understood but all feared. They knew the maps from the newspaper, the radio broadcasts, the casualty counts. But those were numbers. Abstract. Now, war had a face. *Their* face. *His*.

When they sat down to dinner, there was a moment where everything felt almost normal. Plates clinked, butter passed, voices rose and fell in familiar cadences. His sisters argued over who had to say grace. All sitting together, his brothers fidgeted with the silverware. His mother fussed over whether the greens were too salty. And Thomas, for a moment, let himself pretend. Pretend that this was just another Sunday night, that he'd wake tomorrow and head to the fields or the feed store instead of the bus depot.

But beneath the small talk and smiles, the truth pulsed like a second heartbeat. His mother's eyes glistened every time she looked at him too long. She kept reaching for her glass, only to set it down untouched. His father cleared his throat twice, then again, shifting in his seat, his fork moving food around more than eating it. No one said it aloud, but they all knew this might be the last meal they shared like this. As a whole family. As *this* version of themselves.

They cleared the dishes and tidied up the kitchen before heading into the living room. Even though they had prepared the fireplace, they hadn't lit it—it was too warm—but they still gathered around it out of habit, just like so many nights before. They talked—but only about small things. Nothing important. The kind of talk that dances around sadness without ever saying it out loud. Sometimes a quiet pause would fall between them, thick with unspoken thoughts. But

Thomas didn't mind. He sat there, just listening. The soft tap of his father's fingers on the armrest, his mother's gentle voice, and his sisters quietly arguing over who would do the dishes tomorrow.

He would miss this. All of it. In a way, he couldn't even explain.

As the clock crept past ten, the family peeled away. His sisters hugged him tighter than usual—one tucked a folded scrap of paper into his hand, a letter she said not to read until he was on the bus. The brothers all went to bed early, knowing it would be difficult to fall asleep as they thought about Thomas. His mother kissed his cheek without a word, her hand lingering on his shoulder. And his father... well, he gave him a nod. Just a small one. But it was enough. It was everything.

When they were gone, and the house had fallen into the quiet stillness of late evening, Thomas remained. He sat in the old armchair across from his father's, staring out the window at the moonlit fields beyond. The rows of cotton gleamed silver in the night, swaying in the wind. He knew every inch of that land, every tree and fence post. It had raised him.

Rooted him. But now it felt like something he had to let go of.

Tomorrow, he'd board that bus. He'd put Mississippi in his rearview. He would trade the sounds of cicadas and porch swings for drills and ocean spray.

He was terrified. And excited. And more alone than he'd ever felt.

But he also felt something else. A quiet, burning resolve.

His life—the one he had clung to so tightly—was changing. Jeremiah's memory pressed against his chest like a heartbeat. His family's love filled the room even in their absence. And out there, beyond the cotton fields and riverbanks, an entire world waited.

He took one last look out the window, then rose, steadying himself.

Tomorrow, everything would begin.

Early the next morning, long before the sun broke the

horizon, the family gathered in the soft blue hush of pre-dawn. The old car sat waiting in the gravel drive, dew glistening on its faded hood. The air was thick and still, wrapped in the cool dampness that only came in those quiet Mississippi mornings. Not a rooster crowed, not a dog barked. Even the cicadas had gone silent, as if the world itself was holding its breath.

No one spoke much as they loaded into the car. Thomas sat in the back between his sisters and brothers; his knees pressed against the worn seat in front of him. With her Bible in her lap, his mother's fingers moved along its cracked leather spine. His father turned the key, and the engine sputtered to life with a familiar rattle, coughing smoke into the cool morning air. They pulled away from the house; the tires crunching over the gravel like footsteps leaving home.

The drive to Jackson was two hours, and for most of it, the silence held. Not an uncomfortable silence—but a reverent one, thick with emotion, too big for words. They lowered the windows, letting in a breeze carrying the scent of wet earth, pine trees, and distant wood smoke. Thomas stared out at the fields and forests, memorizing everything as they passed. From the trees, the moss hung like lace. The white clapboard churches. The rusting water towers painted with town names that always felt too small for the size of the grief he was carrying.

Every mile felt like a goodbye.

He caught glimpses of familiar places: the old gas station where he and Jeremiah used to sneak colas on hot summer days, the bend in the road where they'd once chased fireflies barefoot through the grass, the rail crossing they'd dared each other to jump before the train came. The memories rose like ghosts, vivid and aching.

He wanted to remember it all—not just for himself, but for Jeremiah, too. He wanted to carry this place with him, to keep it alive in the stories he would tell far from here.

By the time they reached the edge of Jackson, the sky had shifted to a pale lavender. The bus station came into view slowly, rising behind a row of warehouses, its brick facade plain and functional. But the Navy bus, parked at the curb, was impossible to miss. It sat like a sentinel in the morning light—dull blue paint, wide windows fogged from within, its engine rumbling with low anticipation. A few other cars, already parked nearby, had families spilling out onto the sidewalk in hushed, uncertain movements.

Young men stood in small groups—some in quiet conversation, others pacing, duffel bags slung over shoulders, eyes darting toward the horizon like they were searching for answers in the sky. Mothers clung to sons. Fathers gave stiff nods and bracing pats on the back. There was laughter, but it was brittle, edged with something that might have been fear. The air was thick with the bitter-sweetness of departure—the electric tension between pride and heartbreak.

Thomas's family climbed out of the car. His mother's hands trembled as she smoothed his collar and tried to keep her voice steady. Her eyes, red from a night of little sleep, never left her face.

She pulled him into a tight embrace, pressing her cheek against his chest, her whisper lost in the engine's sound. *"Lord keep him. Let him come home."* It wasn't just a prayer—it was a plea. A mother's final offering.

His father stepped forward next, his shoulders squared and

eyes shining with something he refused to let fall. He reached out, gripped Thomas's hand in a firm shake, then pulled him into a quick, hard hug. When he stepped back, his voice was low and steady.

"Make us proud, son."

No elaboration. No fanfare. Just the words Thomas had been waiting to hear his entire life. He nodded; his throat too tight for a reply.

His sisters didn't pretend to be strong. They clung to him, arms looped around his waist like if they held tight enough, they might keep him from going. Their tears came fast and hot, soaking through the fabric of his shirt. One of them slipped a small handkerchief into his pocket, embroidered with his initials. He didn't say nothing—he just squeezed her hand, feeling the weight of every childhood memory passed between them.

All five of his brothers circled him and gave him a group bear hug. Tears in their eyes as they wished Thomas the best and they let loose. The brothers joined the rest of the family as they all waved goodbye.

And then the bus door creaked open.

The driver—an older man with a cigarette tucked behind one ear—called out names from a clipboard, his voice slicing through the morning fog like a bell toll. Thomas's name was near the end. When it came, everything seemed to blur.

He looked at his family one last time—burned their faces into his mind.

Then he turned, hoisted his bag onto his shoulder, and climbed aboard.

The door hissed shut behind him with a finality that made his heart skip. He found a seat near the window and stared out at the people he loved, watching as they stood close together, waving, crying, holding on to one another.

The bus lurched forward.

As Jackson faded into the distance, and the road unwound before him like a ribbon stretched toward something unknown, Thomas kept his hand tucked over his heart, where the handkerchief lay, soft and warm.

He didn't know where he was going or what waited for him beyond the next hill, the next ocean.

But he knew who he was leaving for. And that would have to be enough.

For now.

The journey to Camp Robert Smalls at Great Lakes, Illinois, was a long and grueling one. Young men crowded the bus, most of whom were as nervous and uncertain as Thomas. They were all leaving something behind—families, homes, dreams—for the promise of something unknown. The seats were uncomfortable, the suspension nonexistent, and the hours seemed to stretch on. They stopped at small towns along the way to refuel and stretch their legs, but the journey was a blur of endless roads and restless thoughts.

At night, men filled the bus with the sound of their letter-writing to loved ones. Thomas, too, scribbled notes to his family, trying to put into words what he was feeling. It was harder than he thought. How do you explain the jumble of emotions inside you—excitement, fear, hope, and homesickness—all tangled together? How do you tell the people you love that you don't know if you'll ever see them again?

During one of the long, dusty stops, the Navy bus pulled into a rural depot just outside of Memphis, Tennessee. The sun hung high, casting sharp shadows across the gravel lot, and the air was thick with heat and the faint scent of diesel. Recruits stretched their legs, wandered toward vending machines or shaded porches, and stood around smoking or chatting in quiet groups. There was a sense of shared purpose in the air, but also a nervous energy—each man, in his own way, aware that this journey was a step toward something they couldn't quite grasp.

As Thomas stepped off the bus and stretched his back, he noticed, for the first time, two black men seated at the very rear. They had been there since the beginning—he was sure of it now—but they had spoken little, hadn't mingled with the rest of the group. They kept their heads down, their voices low, their presence nearly invisible except to those who were looking.

Slowly rising, they waited until the others had dispersed, then moved together toward the back of the station, where they saw a faded wooden sign hanging crooked above the doorway: COLORED ONLY. And it hit Thomas harder than he expected.

He watched as the two men disappeared around the corner, their shoulders hunched, careful not to make a scene, not to draw attention. It was muscle memory—survival passed down like scripture. They moved like men used to being watched, judged, punished for simply existing in the wrong space.

Thomas shifted his weight, suddenly uncomfortable. He had grown up with signs like that. With split entrances at diners and different water fountains at the courthouse. It had always been part of the world he knew, part of the air he breathed in Mississippi. His family talked very little about it. It just *was*—like the heat or the kudzu or the Sunday sermon. But now, here, standing on the edge of adulthood and war, something about it unsettled him in a new way.

They were all heading to the same place. Wearing the same uniform. Training with the same rifles. Their superiors would order them to fight and die for the same flag. But those two men couldn't even walk through the same door as the rest of them.

He glanced around at the other white recruits. Some didn't seem to notice. Others, if they did, didn't care. A few even smirked, muttering jokes under their breath that made Thomas's stomach twist.

He thought they would send everyone overseas, but some would still have to bow their heads at home.

He looked back toward the "Colored Only" sign and felt a twinge of shame. Not because he had done anything—but because he hadn't. Because he never had. Not when Jeremiah was alive. The town had looked the other way, not then. Not when people whispered hate like it was just part of the weather.

And yet those two men still climbed aboard the same bus. Still wore the same boots. Still marched toward war with a quiet dignity that shamed the ones who laughed at them.

Thomas wondered what it felt like—to be asked to lay your life down for a country that wouldn't let you sit at the same lunch counter. To fight for freedoms that were denied to you. What kind of faith did that take? What kind of courage?

As the bus rumbled to life again and they all climbed back aboard, Thomas took a slower glance toward the rear. One of the black recruits met his gaze—just for a second. No words passed between them. Just a nod. A small, solemn acknowledgment. And Thomas nodded back, heart heavy with thoughts he hadn't had the words for yet.

He sat back in his seat and stared out the window as the landscape rolled by, his reflection dimmed in the glass. The world outside was wide and open—but the divisions within it felt as deep as ever.

Still, something had shifted in him.

He didn't know what he would do about it yet. But he knew one thing for certain—when he stepped into that uniform, he was going to carry more than just his own story. He would carry Jeremiah. He would carry those two men. His burden would be the weight of a promise, quiet yet unshakable:

If I come back, I won't stay silent anymore.

After two long days on the road, the bus pulled into Camp Robert Smalls. Thomas stepped off the bus, his legs stiff and sore, and took in his new surroundings. The air was cooler here, crisp and clean, a stark contrast to the thick humidity of Mississippi. The camp was a flurry of activity, with men rushing about, barking orders, and the distant sound of drills being called. This was it. Basic training.

The first few days at Camp Robert Smalls were a blur of physical exams, paperwork, and nonstop briefings. They placed Thomas, along with the other new recruits, into a training unit. His assigned role: Gunner's Mate. It was a job with a lot of responsibility. His training would teach him how to use and take care of the ship's weapons—guns, torpedoes, and ammunition. The idea of working with such powerful equipment made him feel both excited and a little nervous.

Training was grueling. The days started early, before the sun had even risen, with physical drills that pushed Thomas to his limits. He had always been strong, growing up working the fields and fishing by the river, but this was different. The instructors were relentless, demanding perfection in every movement, every action. The classroom instruction was just as intense, filled with technical details about weaponry, navigation, and safety protocols. Sometimes Thomas wondered if he would make it through.

But he wasn't alone. The camaraderie among the recruits was unlike anything Thomas had ever experienced. They were all in this together, enduring the same hardships, sharing the same fears. Over time, they became a second family to Thomas, bound by the shared goal of serving their country. At night, after a long day of training, they would sit in their bunks, talking about their homes, their families, and the lives they had left behind. Thomas found solace in those moments, knowing that he wasn't the only one struggling to balance the weight of duty with the ache of homesickness.

One night, as they sat around talking, one of the black recruits, a man named George, shared his own story. He talked about growing up in the South, not unlike Thomas, but with far more challenges. He spoke of the discrimination he faced daily, of being relegated to menial tasks even here, in the military. His words were quiet, but they carried a weight that Thomas couldn't ignore. The situation reminded them of their world—a world where not everyone had equality, even while preparing for a common cause.

Thomas found himself growing more determined with each passing day. The training was brutal, but he gritted his teeth and pushed forward, knowing it was preparing him for the harsh realities of war. He learned to operate the ship's guns with precision, to handle ammunition with care, to work alongside his fellow sailors as a cohesive unit. The challenges were many, but Thomas faced them head-on, driven by a sense of duty and the memory of those he had left behind.

As the weeks turned into months, Thomas grew stronger— both physically and mentally. He had come to Camp Robert Smalls as a young man unsure of his place in the world, but he was leaving it as a sailor, ready to face whatever lay ahead. The actual test, he knew, was still to come. The war was waiting, and with it, the true test of everything he had learned.

On the last night before they were to leave for deployment, Thomas lay in his bunk, staring up at the ceiling. He thought of his family, of Jeremiah, of the river he had left behind. The path ahead was uncertain, but one thing was clear—he was ready. Ready to serve, ready to fight, ready to protect the people and the country he loved. Whatever challenges lay ahead, Thomas knew he would face them with the same determination that had brought him here.

He had come a long way from the banks of the Chickasawhay River, but no matter how far he traveled, that river, and the memories it held, would always be with him.

Thomas's time in the Navy was full of challenges and life-changing moments. What started as months of training quickly will turn into years of service. During that time, many experiences left a lasting mark on him, helping shape the man—and sailor—he would become.

Thomas and his crew found themselves in one of the largest and most important naval battles of World War II, the Battle of Leyte Gulf in the Pacific, creating one of their most unforgettable moments. This battle would test their courage, strength, and teamwork like never before.

After months of training as a Gunner's mate, they assigned Thomas to the USS Birmingham, a light cruiser, in 1944. The navy sent his ship to the Pacific to help protect the larger fleet. The *Birmingham* was part of the U.S. Navy's Seventh Fleet, which played a big role in the fight against Japan. Their mission was to help take back the Philippines—a key part of General Douglas MacArthur's promise to return to the islands. It would lead to one of the biggest and most important battles between the U.S. Navy and the Japanese Navy.

As the fleet moved toward the Philippines, Thomas did not know that he was heading into one of the biggest and most intense naval battles in history. The Battle of Leyte Gulf took place over several days in late October 1944. It involved hundreds of ships and planes and became a major turning point in the war in the Pacific.

Thomas's heart pounded as they received the orders for engagement. The crew perpetually drilled, and Thomas honed his knowledge of the ship's weapons systems to perfection during long hours of practice. Yet nothing could truly prepare a sailor for the reality of combat. This would be the first time Thomas would see actual battle at sea—real battle, real danger, real lives at stake.

As Thomas manned his post, the first waves of Japanese attacks began with aerial bombardment and kamikaze strikes. Planes screeched across the sky, their engines roaring thunderingly as the air buzzed with activity. The alarm sounded across the deck, and men scrambled to their stations. The ship's gun batteries came to life, and Thomas, stationed at the main 5-inch dual-purpose guns, could feel the energy and tension in the air.

Enemy planes targeted American ships as they swooped low, their bombs screaming toward the water. Thomas's hands were steady on the firing controls, but his heart raced as the ship's anti-aircraft guns exploded into action. The sky lit up with tracers and explosions, and Tom's team fired round after round, trying to fend off the enemy aircraft that seemed to materialize out of the sun.

Thomas shouted commands to the crew working the ammo below deck as the team loaded shells, their movements practiced and efficient. With urgency, the crew passed each shell, and Thomas shouted every order above the din of battle. He focused on the incoming waves of planes, their silhouettes darting in and out of clouds of smoke.

"FIRE!" the command echoed, and the deck shuddered as the ship's guns erupted. The first Japanese plane was hit, spiraling down into the ocean in a fiery ball of smoke and flame. As another aircraft dived toward their ship and released a bomb, Thomas gasped; the bomb narrowly missed, exploding in the water near the hull. The shockwave rocked the vessel, spraying saltwater across the deck and knocking several men off their feet.

Thomas had heard of Kamikaze pilots before, but he didn't truly understand what it meant—until he saw it with his own eyes. These pilots flew their planes straight into American ships on purpose, knowing they would die. Their goal was to cause as much damage as possible by turning their planes into flying bombs. One of those planes targeted the *Birmingham*. Thomas watched in shock and fear as it came closer, the engine screaming so vociferously; it drowned out every other sound.

"Incoming! Brace yourselves!" someone shouted.

Thomas's body tensed; his hands frozen for a split second before he resumed firing. The guns roared, spitting fire into the sky, and at the last moment, they hit the kamikaze plane. It exploded mid-air, debris raining down into the ocean. But there was no time to breathe a sigh of relief. More planes were on the way.

By the second day, the battle had grown even more intense. The Japanese had sent out every ship they had left, including their last aircraft carriers. Fighting became more direct, with ships like the *Birmingham* helping protect the larger battleships from attacks coming from all sides. On the surface of the water, destroyers and battleships fired powerful blasts at each other, shaking the sea with their force.

Thomas's hands shook with exhaustion, but he forced himself to keep going. There was no room for hesitation— his crew depended on him. His team stacked the ammunition high as they worked tirelessly to keep the guns loaded. Above them, the whine of incoming Japanese dive bombers sliced through the air. Every muscle in his body ached from the constant action, but the adrenaline that pumped through his veins kept him focused.

One of the worst moments of the battle occurred when a Japanese bomb hit the USS Princeton, the Birmingham's sister ship. The explosion sent plumes of black smoke into the air, and Thomas could see flames licking the deck of the carrier in the distance. The Princeton was in grave danger of sinking, and despite the ongoing engagement, the Birmingham steamed toward her to offer assistance.

As Thomas and the others rushed to help fight fires and evacuate the wounded from the *Princeton*, a second, even larger explosion shook the damaged carrier. This blast was massive—it tore apart much of the ship. Pieces of the *Princeton* flew through the air, and the powerful shockwave slammed into the *Birmingham*. The impact was deadly. The blast killed over 200 sailors on Thomas's ship and injured hundreds more. Thomas was among the injured, thrown hard against a wall by the force of the blast.

Thomas was stunned, his ears ringing and his vision swimming. When he regained his bearings, he looked around in horror. The deck was a scene of utter devastation— mangled bodies, blood, and twisted steel. Thomas staggered to his feet, trying to shake off the dizziness, and joined the efforts to tend to the wounded. The cries of injured sailors filled the air, and the acrid smell of burning fuel was thick in his nose. The damage to the Birmingham was severe, but the ship remained afloat.

Even in the chaos, Thomas's training kicked in. He assisted the medics, helping to carry the wounded below deck. His head ached from where he had hit it, and his hands shook from the shock of the blast, but he pushed on. There were too many men to save, too many lives on the line. As the battle raged around him, Thomas thought of his family back home, of the river, of Jeremiah. He had never felt closer to death.

The next day, the tide began to turn. Despite the tremendous losses and the devastation caused by the kamikaze attacks, the U.S. Navy had gained the upper hand. Thomas's ship, though damaged, continued to fight alongside the fleet, pouring everything they had into the battle.

The Japanese fleet, badly damaged, made one last desperate attempt to fight back. But the U.S. forces were powerful and determined, stopping each attack. Thomas and his crew were tired, but they didn't give up. They stayed at their stations, firing their guns through the final hours of the battle. Every shot felt heavier, every explosion louder, as the long fight moved toward its end.

By the end of the fourth day, it was clear: the U.S. Navy had dealt the Imperial Japanese Navy a devastating blow. The Battle of Leyte Gulf marked the end of their ability to fight effectively at sea. The U.S. Navy had won, and with that victory, the road to retaking the Philippines was clear.

Thomas stood on the deck of the *Birmingham*, staring out over the waters of the Pacific, now quiet after the days of battle. The sun was setting, casting a warm orange glow over the ocean, and the air smelled of salt and gunpowder. The adrenaline had worn off, and all that remained was the exhaustion—the bone-deep weariness that only comes after days of fighting for your life. He looked around at his fellow sailors, many of them limping, bandaged, or bruised. They had survived, but the cost had been great.

As the ship limped back to port for repairs, Thomas's thoughts drifted again to Mississippi, to the river, to the life he had left behind. He had faced death and destruction in ways he never imagined. He had seen men give their lives for their country, and he had watched friends fall. But through it all, he had found a strength within himself that he hadn't known existed. The boy who had once fished by the river had become a man, shaped by war, but not yet broken by it.

Thomas would return to battle many times after Leyte, but in that particular fight, the sound of kamikazes and the explosion of the *Princeton* would haunt him for the rest of his days. That battle—its bravery, loss, and brotherhood—

seared itself into his mind, as deeply as the Chickasawhay Riverbanks of his childhood. It was a battle that defined not only the course of the war but also the man Thomas had become.

Chapter 3

The Pull of Home

The cold, briny breeze rolling in off Puget Sound wrapped itself around Thomas like a second uniform as he stepped off the gangway, the metal thudding beneath his boots as he touched solid ground for the first time in weeks. Days of the ship's unrelenting sway had left him disoriented; the sudden stillness of the land felt both unnatural and profound, relieving, like waking from a long, uneasy sleep.

Around him, the Seattle docks buzzed with motion and noise. Cranes creaked and groaned as they hoisted crates from cargo holds; sailors shouted to one another over the din of unloading supplies and the hiss of steam from nearby engines. The gulls wheeled above the ships, crying out over the clatter of the busy port like hecklers from the sky. Men in peacoats and dungarees moved like clockwork, carrying boxes, orders, stories from far-off waters.

But Thomas stood still, his eyes scanning the horizon beyond the hulls and the haze.

Seattle.

He'd passed through once, earlier in the war—barely enough time to stretch his legs before shipping out again. Back then, it had been a blur of gray skies and sea salt, a quick breath before the plunge. But this time... this time was different.

As the sound of the sea faded behind him, the city unfolded ahead like something imagined. Just beyond the dockyards, Pike Place Market spilled into the streets in a riot of color and sound. Vendors barked about the day's catch—salmon, halibut, shrimp still twitching in their crates. Bouquets of tulips and peonies burst in bright pinks and yellows beside stalls of handmade soaps, preserves, and carved wooden toys. The scent of roasted coffee drifted from a nearby cafe, mixing with the salt air in a way that felt foreign and wonderful.

It was chaos—but a kind of chaos that pulsed with purpose. With possibility.

Thomas tucked his hands into the deep pockets of his coat and moved slowly into the current of people, taking it all in. The streets were alive in a way Mississippi never had been.

Back home, life moved at the speed of porch swings and Sunday sermons. It was slow, deliberate, and always watching. There, the heat clung to you like judgment, and you could hear your own footsteps echo down the dusty roads. But here—here the air was sharp and electric. It smelled of ocean and engines and something else, something Thomas couldn't name just yet. Something that felt like freedom.

As he wandered further into the city, he found himself drawn to the rhythm of it all—the way people flowed around each other, how the city seemed to welcome strangers without asking where they came from. No one knew his name here. No one knew about Jeremiah, or the hanging tree, or the quiet way his family had hugged him goodbye at that bus station back in Jackson. Here, he was just another sailor in a sea of wool coats and white caps.

"But Seattle gave Thomas more than just a place to disappear—it gave him something he didn't even know he needed: a fresh start."

He didn't know what it meant yet. He didn't know if he'd ever make a home here, or if he'd even get the chance. The war was still out there, swallowing boys whole, and every ship he boarded might be his last. But as he stood in the shadow of the fish market, watching life burst from every stall and every doorway, Thomas felt it—the pull. Not just of a city, but of a future.

He could almost hear Jeremiah's voice in his ear, low and teasing: *"See, Tommy? Told you there was more out there."*

Thomas closed his eyes for a brief second and let the breeze hit his face full on. The salt stung, but it was a good kind of sting—sharp, real, alive. He took a long breath, as if trying to pull the entire city into his lungs.

Pike Place Market's vibrant tapestry—people moving, colors splashing from produce and flowers—filled Thomas's view. He noticed a figure near a flower stall. She stood just off to the side, thumbing through a bouquet of daffodils with a delicate, thoughtful motion. Her dark hair, thick and wavy, caught the breeze and danced around her shoulders, framing a face that seemed both luminous and grounded, like she belonged in the landscape yet somehow stood apart from it.

And then—she looked up.

Their eyes met, and for a heartbeat, the entire market fell away. The clamor of the fishmongers, the shouted prices, the clang of crates and footsteps—all of it faded until there was only her. Something ancient and instinctual pulled at Thomas's chest. Before he could talk himself out of it, he found his feet moving forward, as if carried by the wind itself.

"Excuse me, miss," he said, voice steady but thick with the unmistakable drawl of Mississippi, "I couldn't help but notice you. Do you live around here?"

The woman turned to face him. For a breath, surprise flickered in her eyes—but only for a breath. Then came the smile. Slow, warm, effortless. It bloomed across her face like morning sun through a cloudy sky.

"Yes," she said, her voice smooth and grounded, touched with a Northwestern lilt. I'm Betty. Seattle is where I've spent all of my life.

"I'm Thomas," he replied, adjusting his posture as he stood

before her in his Navy blues. He felt a little foolish now—he hadn't planned what to say, hadn't approached a woman like this before. But Betty's steady gaze and open smile disarmed him. She didn't seem put off or hurried. She just waited.

Soon, they walked side by side through the market, winding past stalls bursting with rhubarb and radishes, tulips and lavender, fresh loaves of bread stacked like treasure. Their conversation started with small things—the weather, the city, his first impressions of Seattle—but something about the cadence of her voice, the unhurried way she spoke, made it easy for Thomas to open up.

They stopped for lunch at a small cafe nestled above the market, its windows overlooking Elliott Bay. They chose a table near the glass; the view stretching wide and glimmering under the early afternoon sun. Betty ordered black coffee and a sandwich; Thomas went for clam chowder and warm bread.

As they ate, the conversation deepened.

He spoke of Mississippi—not with nostalgia, but with reverence. The smell of honeysuckle at dusk, the feel of river clay between his toes as a boy, the slow churn of the seasons. He told her about joining the Navy, how the war had pulled him into a world he never imagined. And though he didn't plan to, he found himself speaking of Jeremiah—of loss, of anger, of the quiet grief that had shaped everything since.

Betty didn't interrupt. She didn't pry. She just listened, her hands wrapped around her coffee cup; her eyes fixed on his with a gentle intensity that made it easy to keep talking.

She spoke next, describing her upbringing. From the age of six, when her parents gave her up, she lived in a brick orphanage on the edge of Queen Anne Hill. She talked about the harsh winters and rigid rules, but also the small acts of kindness that helped her get through it—like the cook giving her extra food and the librarian letting her borrow more books. She said she built her life by learning to rely on herself, finding joy in simple things, and always looking ahead.

The quiet resilience struck Thomas—not bitterness, not self-pity. Just truth. Clean and unvarnished.

They spent the rest of the day wandering through the city

like old friends rediscovering it together. At one of the tallest buildings in Seattle, they climbed the stairs to the top and stood side by side, the entire city stretching out beneath them like a promise. The sun, now sliding low in the sky, cast golden light across the sound, painting the ships and rooftops in burnished hues.

"It's beautiful," Thomas said, not taking his eyes off the horizon.

"It is," Betty agreed. "But it's more beautiful today."

He looked at her then, and for the first time in a long time, he felt something break open inside—a possibility found a place to land.

They continued to the Japanese Tea Garden as twilight began to settle in. The garden was hushed, held in shadows and soft light, the wind moving through the trees in gentle sighs. They walked slowly, pausing at the koi pond to watch the fish gliding beneath the surface like living brushstrokes. Neither of them spoke much here. They didn't need to. There was something sacred in the quiet between them.

As night fell, they boarded a ferry crossing Puget Sound, the hum of the motor vibrating beneath their feet as they stood together at the bow. The wind had picked up, cool and sharp, tugging at their jackets. Lights flickered across the water from distant boats, and behind them, Seattle shimmered like a city made of glass and starlight.

Thomas turned to Betty, his hand brushing hers. "This was… more than I expected."

She smiled, pulling her coat tighter around her. "Me too."

They stood that way for a long time, eyes fixed on the water, the space between them slowly closing.

When the returning ferry docked and they stepped onto the creaking wooden planks, neither wanted to say goodbye. The world felt heavier again, the weight of war waiting just around the corner.

"I have to go back," Thomas said quietly, his voice low with regret. "My ship's leaving in two hours."

"I know," Betty replied. Her expression didn't falter, though her eyes held something deep and shining.

He hesitated, then took her hands in his. "I don't know when, but I'll come back. I promise."

For a moment, the wind died, and the world stood still.

"I'll be here," she said.

And with that, he turned and walked into the night—one foot on the dock, the other still lingering on the deck of something new.

With those simple words, Thomas returned to his ship. But something inside him had changed. The sea, which had always been a source of adventure and freedom, now felt empty without Betty. As the ship pulled away from the dock, Seattle fading into the horizon, Thomas stood at the railing, his thoughts filled with her.

Thomas would spend the next few weeks enduring some of the most grueling and difficult times of his life. The sea stretched out endlessly in every direction, a flat, indifferent expanse of steel-gray water that seemed to swallow time itself. Days blurred into a routine of drills, maintenance, and endless watches. The sun rose and set with mechanical regularity, offering no distinction between Monday or Sunday, joy or sorrow. Salt clung to everything—his skin, his clothes, his very breath—and the constant groan of the ship's hull became as familiar as his own heartbeat.

Sleep was light and broken. Meals were often cold and rushed. Letters were promised but rarely delivered on time. Most days, Thomas kept his head down and did what needed doing, but every now and then, when the loneliness settled in too thick, he'd steal a quiet moment to close his eyes and picture her.

Betty.

Her name alone was enough to bring warmth into the cold metal corridors of the ship. He thought of her every time he looked out over the rail at sunset, when the sky exploded in brilliant pinks and oranges that mirrored the day they stood on the ferry, the wind in her hair. He could still remember the exact sound of her laugh when he mispronounced "bouquet" at the flower stall, the way she had tilted her head and said, "You sure you're not a poet, sailor?" Her voice had nestled itself into the back of his mind, and some days, it was the only thing that kept him steady.

He wrote to her as often as time allowed—sometimes after his shift, sometimes scribbling in the dim light before reveille. He filled the pages with stories from the ship: of sleeping in cramped quarters below deck, of the camaraderie that had bloomed between the men, and of the strange, distant lands they passed without ever setting foot on shore. But more than that, he wrote about *her*. About how he missed her. About how her memory softened the sharp edges of sea life. He wrote with a kind of honesty he had never been able to share back home—words he hadn't even known he carried until they poured out onto the page.

The mail came sporadically, always in bundled deliveries when they docked in a friendly port or crossed paths with a supply vessel. Most of the time, Thomas came back to his bunk with empty hands. But one quiet evening, after a day of engine work that left his arms aching and his face slick with sweat, he returned to his berth to find a single white envelope resting on his pillow.

For a moment, he just stared at it.

Betty wrote his name in delicate, looping script. His hands trembled as he picked it up. The paper was soft, the kind you didn't find in Navy post exchanges, and the faintest trace of her perfume still clung to it, lavender and lemon, like the ghost of summer.

He sat down on the edge of his bunk, closed his eyes, and inhaled. And then, carefully, he tore it open.

Her words enveloped him like a blanket. She wrote of the rain in Seattle—how it painted the sidewalks silver and made the market smell of wet wood and crushed petals. Curled in their favorite cafe, she told him how she'd taken to evening reading, saving him a seat across from her despite his absence. Despite her discussion of the war and its pervasive effects, her focus unavoidably reverted to him. *You're the brightest part of my day, Thomas. I think about you every night before I fall asleep.*

He read the letter three times before he folded it carefully and tucked it into his jacket pocket, right over his heart.

Those letters—hers and his in return—became his lifeline. They were more than paper and ink. They were proof that something good still existed in the world, that beyond the endless sea and the threat of distant gunfire, there was someone waiting for him. Someone who saw past the uniform and the war, who saw *him.*

He wrote back the same night, filling every inch of the page with longing, gratitude, and promise. At night, from the deck, he told her of stars brighter than any in Mississippi, and how he pretended she was there, seeing the same sky. His vision of their future together included a small house with a garden, Sunday mornings spent with music and tea, and perhaps even children who resembled her. He didn't know when— or even if—it would happen, but he had to believe in something.

He had to believe in her.

And so, as the days wore on and the ship pressed further into uncharted waters, Thomas kept her letters folded in his jacket. He touched them before each shift. He reread them in the moments before sleep claimed him. In a world that had lost so much certainty, Betty became his compass.

She was his shore.

And no matter where the war took him, he was already charting a course back to her.

When the Korean War broke out in 1950, Thomas was older, seasoned, and no longer the wide-eyed young man who had first enlisted during World War II. He had already seen what war could do—how it wore down a man's spirit, how it could twist time into something jagged and cruel. He'd hoped, perhaps, that his days of battle were behind him. But history had other plans, and before long, he found himself thrust once more into the thick of chaos—back on the sea, back in uniform, back in a world where each sunrise was a gamble.

This time, the waters didn't offer him solace. The ocean that had once whispered of freedom and new beginnings now churned with the dark weight of conflict. Over the Sea of Japan, smoke and tension frequently darkened the skies. The ship groaned with the strain of war—metal vibrating with each maneuver, the decks slick with salt and sweat, radios crackling with orders that sent men into harm's way.

Brutal fighting characterized the battles. Each engagement brought with it a fresh wave of casualties, the sharp staccato of gunfire punctuated by the cries of the wounded and the eerie silence that followed the fallen. Thomas had seen many young men come aboard with fire in their hearts, only to leave in flag-draped coffins—or worse, not at all. He had helped carry more than one stretcher, had pressed his hands against wounds that wouldn't stop bleeding, had held dog tags with trembling fingers, reading names he'd joked with only days before.

Every death was a weight added to his soul, a burden he carried in the quiet hours after the guns had gone silent. He fought undaunted, — because there was no other choice. He performed his duties with a calm that others mistook for fearlessness, but inside, he was just trying to stay afloat, to keep from drowning in it all.

Thomas received awards—silver bars, ribbons, and letters of praise—but none of them meant as much to him as the light blue envelopes that showed up now and then from Seattle. Each one was from Betty.

Her letters were soft shields against the violence of the world. They were full of warmth and minor stories: how the market had expanded, how a neighbor's dog had gone missing and then come back with a kitten in its mouth, how she'd taken up painting again. She never wrote about the war—never asked about blood or battles. Instead, she wrote about *home*. The home she was waiting to build with him.

He carried her words close, tucked in the inside pocket of his coat, wrapped in waxed paper to keep them dry. Sometimes, in the dead of night, when sleep wouldn't come, he'd unfold one and read by the faint glow of a red-tinted flashlight, his lips mouthing the words as if saying them aloud could bring her closer. *Come back to me,* she'd written once. *Come back and let's make something beautiful from all this pain.*

Those words anchored him. Gave him something to believe in when so much around him seemed senseless.

When the war finally ended and the Navy released him from duty in 1953, Thomas stood on the dock in San Diego, duffel slung over his shoulder, the world ultimately quiet again— but filled with questions. He had made it through. Somehow. But what now?

The Navy offered to keep him on—higher rank, better pay, a future in uniform. Mississippi waited too, with its slow drawl and familiar dirt roads, its porch swings and front-yard magnolias. His parents were older now. His sisters had children of their own. It was home. The place where his story had begun.

But then there was Seattle.

Betty.

She had written to him just two weeks before: *I'm still here, Thomas. I'm still waiting. The room is ready. The kettle's on the stove. Come home to me.*

He sat with that choice for days, carrying it around like a coin in his pocket. One side glittered with comfort and roots, the other with risk and love. Mississippi would always be a part of him. But when he closed his eyes, it wasn't the riverbanks or the cotton fields he saw.

It was Betty's smile at the flower stall.

Her fingers brushing his across a ferry rail.

The sound of her voice promising a future in a city that had once whispered to him like a promise in the wind.

And so, Thomas chose love.

He boarded a northbound train with nothing but his duffel and a pocket full of letters. As the landscape changed—from deserts to forests, mountains to misty coasts—he felt something inside him gradually begin to heal. He was going home.

Not to the past.

But to the future.

To Betty.

To the life they had dreamed of in the shadows of war.

To the peace they had earned.

When Thomas returned to Seattle, the city felt different— not because it had changed, but because *he* had. Years weighed on him, marked by the war's scars, but the sight of

Betty at the station, daffodils mirroring their first day, lifted that weight slightly. Her smile was still the same. So was the warmth in her eyes. And it was there, on a quiet morning with the salty wind from the Sound rolling in behind them, that Thomas took her hands in his and asked, simply, fervently, *"Will you marry me?"*

She didn't hesitate. Her *yes* was quiet, but full of promise. In that moment, the noise of the world faded once again— just as it had the day they met.

Betty had a son from a previous relationship—a shy, dark-eyed boy named Ron, who was six years old and more curious than talkative. At first, Thomas didn't know how to be a father to someone else's child, especially one who had already seen his fair share of upheaval. But he made a quiet vow to himself to *try*, to be steady, to show up, even when he didn't know precisely how.

The three of them packed their modest belongings and left Seattle behind, chasing a dream of fresh beginnings in California. They settled in the misty, redwood-covered hills of the Santa Cruz Mountains, where the trees reached high into the sky and the coastal fog rolled in like a slow tide each morning. Thomas took a job in the dairy industry—early mornings, hard labor, dependable pay. He rose with the sun and came home smelling of hay and sweat on his clothes. It wasn't glamorous work, but it was honest. And for the first time in a long time, his life felt anchored.

They made a home there—a tiny house tucked into the hillside, flanked by redwoods and wildflowers, with a porch that overlooked the valley below. It was quiet. Peaceful. And full of the sound of life growing.

Their family expanded swiftly. First came *Thomas Jr.*, a strong, spirited boy who carried his father's stubborn streak and his mother's sharp wit. Then *Susan*, with her wild curls and boundless curiosity. Then *James*, quiet and thoughtful, who liked to sit beside Thomas while he worked in the shed, asking endless questions about tools and maps and engines.

And then came *Robert*.

Robert's birth was hard. Something had gone wrong—a spike in fever, an oxygen drop. Betty's labor had been hard, and when the baby was ultimately born, he was listless and silent, his tiny body burning with fever. The nurses whisked him away to the neonatal unit while Thomas stood powerless outside the glass, his knuckles white against the edge of the window, praying to a God he wasn't sure still listened.

Robert stayed in the hospital for weeks. Then months. There were seizures—small at first, then more violent. The doctors warned them gently, then firmly: Robert might never speak. He might never walk. His brain had been damaged, they said, in ways they couldn't entirely explain. The future would be uncertain. And hard.

At home, the family adapted as best they could. The older children swiftly learned how to help—how to soothe their brother when he cried, and how to watch for the signs of an oncoming seizure. Betty never left his side. Thomas, for all his strength, sometimes found himself standing in the hallway at night, weeping silently so no one would hear.

Over time, the responsibility of caring for Robert became more than the family could handle on their own. He needed more help than they could provide—someone to watch him day and night, regular medical attention, and care from trained professionals who understood his condition. The family did their best for as long as they could, but it started to take a toll on everyone. After many long and emotional talks, they made the difficult decision to place him in a care facility nearby. It wasn't a choice they made lightly. It was filled with sadness, guilt, and love. But they knew he would be in a safe place, surrounded by doctors and nurses who could give him the constant care he needed. Even though it was hard to let go, they believed it was the right thing to do for Robert, and for the family.

Leaving him there was the hardest thing they had ever done.

The day they said goodbye; Susan clung to her mother's dress and wouldn't let go. Thomas walked out of the facility feeling like something inside him had cracked wide open, a piece of himself left behind in that sterile, echoing room. Betty didn't speak for most of the ride home. The house felt hollow for weeks afterward.

But they visited often. Brought flowers, toys, songs. Robert, though non-verbal, would sometimes smile when he saw them—a flicker of recognition in his eyes that was more precious than anything.

Through it all, life continued.

The children grew up fast. They climbed trees, caught frogs, came home with report cards and scraped knees. Betty planted roses in the front yard and showed Susan how to bake. Thomas built a small shed out back where he fixed old radios and wrote letters when he needed a break from the noise of the world. Their life was simple—touched by struggle, but filled with love.

And yet, no matter how full his days became, Thomas could never quite shake the homesickness that clung to him like a second skin. Some nights, after the children had gone to bed, he'd sit on the porch with a cup of coffee or a tumbler of bourbon, staring out at the fog as it rolled in through the trees, and imagine the Mississippi nights of his youth. He missed the sound of crickets humming in the tall grass, the fireflies blinking across open fields, the slow creak of a porch swing in the warm, sticky dark. He missed the way the world seemed to move slower back then, like time itself was lazy and kind.

Sometimes, he'd close his eyes and picture Jeremiah's laughter, or his mother's biscuits cooling on the windowsill. He wondered what had become of the riverbank where he and Jeremiah once cast their lines, barefoot and dreaming. A part of him would always belong to Mississippi, to the land that shaped him, even with all its scars.

But as he listened to the wind weaving through the towering redwoods and heard his children's laughter drifting through the open windows, he also knew this life—*this* place—was where he was meant to be.

He had made a choice. And despite the sorrow and the hardship, it had been the right one.

He had chosen love.

He had chosen *family*.

And in doing so, he had found something Mississippi could never quite offer: peace.

As the years rolled on, and the children began to step into their own, the family found themselves once again seeking a new beginning—this time in the quiet beauty of Northern California. They ultimately settled in Burney, a small mountain town nestled among towering pines and was ringed by lakes, rivers, and wilderness trails. It was the kind of place where the air always smelled like pine needles and wood smoke, and the sky at night stretched clear and star-filled over dark forests.

It didn't take long for Thomas and Betty to see the opportunity in the land around them.

Burney Falls, Lake Britton, the rugged expanses of Lassen National Forest surrounded the small town of Burney. People came in droves each summer to fish, hike, and camp. Yet many of them didn't have the time, the know-how, or the inclination to rough it in the wilderness. They wanted nature, yes—but with a little help. And so, with equal parts faith and sweat, Thomas and Betty opened a sporting goods store right off the main road that cut through town. They sold tackle, fishing poles, sleeping bags, maps, lanterns, coolers, and everything a novice or seasoned camper could need.

But it didn't stop there.

Their real innovation—what made them beloved in the community—was the rental and full-service camping experience they offered. Not just a tent and a cooler. Not just a dusty camper trailer. The Smiths made it *easy*. If someone rented a trailer, they didn't have to lift a finger. Thomas, or one of the older kids, would drive it out to the assigned campsite at McArthur-Burney Falls Memorial State Park or one of the nearby lakefront campgrounds. They'd level the trailer, extend the awning, stack firewood near the ring, fill the icebox, and even light a lantern if it was close to nightfall. When a tent was requested, they would meticulously set it up, ensuring it was taut and organized, and the sleeping pads were rolled and prepared.

Also, to enhance the experience, they also rented small fishing boats with motors. So, along with setting up the entire camp, they would deliver a boat to Lake Britten, ready for eager anglers to experience the most of their camping adventure.

When their guests—often city families seeking a peaceful weekend—arrived, all they had to do was step from their car and exhale.

For Thomas, gear was never just about the gear itself. It was about *creating moments*. He had watched too many people live paycheck to paycheck, too tired to plan a getaway, and too overwhelmed by the details to appreciate the surrounding wilderness. His mission was to take the stress out of that, to make *getting away* accessible. He knew from experience— life was short, and family time was precious. If he could make that time easier, more joyful, then he was doing something that mattered.

And the community responded.

The little store, once just a modest idea, quickly became the best in town. Locals came in for tackle and camping tips. Out-of-towners, many from the Bay Area or Sacramento, made it their yearly tradition to rent from the Smiths. Families came back summer after summer, watching their kids grow up against the backdrop of the forest, always greeted by familiar faces and a campsite that felt like home.

It was a true family operation.

Ron was the first to help, using his natural charm and quiet reliability to make deliveries and set up gear. Thomas Jr. took to the logistics like a fish to water, organizing routes, maintenance, and managing supplies. Susan ran the register in the shop and often offered decorating touches—fresh flowers, hand-written welcome notes at the campsites. James, ever curious, handled gear repairs and loved chatting with customers about the trails and the best fishing spots. Even Robert, when he was able to visit with supervision, could light up with joy around the store, watching the hustle and bustle like a silent sentinel.

The business brought them all together, even as they grew and found paths of their own. It grounded them in something shared—something they had built not from capital or convenience, but from love, resilience, and purpose.

But for Thomas, with the success came a certain weight.

He had carried responsibility in war. He had carried grief. Now he carried a different kind of pressure—the knowledge that others depended on him, that this life he had created required constant tending. There were late nights reconciling books. Early mornings loading trailers. Equipment that needed replacing, customers that needed calming. He bore it all, as he always had, but now with more to lose.

And yet, on those evenings when the sun dipped below the ridge and the trees cast long shadows over the hills, Thomas would sit in a folding chair just outside the shop, a thermos of coffee in hand, and listen to the sounds of the town settling into evening. Laughter from a campsite carried on the breeze. A car door shut gently. The scent of pine smoke curled through the air.

He'd think of Mississippi in those moments—the heavy air, the cicadas, the river—and feel that familiar tug of home. But then he'd hear Betty's voice inside, calling from the back room, or see Susan wave as she closed up the register, or watch James hoist a tackle box into the bed of a truck— and he'd smile.

California might not have been where he started, but it had become something just as precious: a legacy, written not in medals or history books, but in fire rings and sleeping bags, in the laughter of children under trees, and in the hearts of those who came to the Smiths for a bit of peace, a bit of wonder.

He had chosen this life. And even in the quiet ache of nostalgia, he knew:

He had chosen well.

Thomas Jr. had a memory that played over and over in his mind, like a favorite movie he couldn't forget. It was the long trips we took across the country to visit my grandparents in Stonewall, Mississippi. It happened during the summer break from school—a time when the sun felt like it never stopped shining, and the days seemed to stretch on forever. But it wasn't just a regular vacation. To me, it felt like an adventure, something special and unforgettable. The long car ride, the changing scenery, the feeling of heading somewhere far away—all of it stayed with me. That trip became a lasting part of my childhood, one of those rare moments that settled deep in my heart and never left.

We were a family of seven packed into our old station wagon, the kind with wood paneling on the sides and windows that had to be cranked down by hand. My father, Thomas, was behind the wheel, as always, with a calm, steady focus that gave the rest of us a sense of safety even when we were hurtling down unfamiliar highways. My mother, *Betty*, sat in the passenger seat with her well-worn Rand McNally Road atlas spread across her lap, dog-eared and marked with handwritten notes—mom's version of GPS.

In the backseat, my sister *Susan* and I jostled for space while my older brother *Ron* lounged by the window, and our younger brother *James* tried his best to fall asleep with his head propped against a pillow wedged between him and the door. We were a tight bunch, elbow to elbow with our snacks, coloring books, and cassette tapes, our laughter rising and falling with the rhythm of the road.

The trip would take four days—four long days that stretched across the spine of America—and we set out that first morning with hearts full of excitement and restless energy. As we pulled away from our home nestled in the Santa Cruz Mountains, we watched the fog rolling over the treetops behind us, knowing that ahead lay 2,000 miles of open road and everything in between.

That first day was filled with wonder. As the familiar landmarks of California fell behind us, the landscape began to shift. Rolling hills shifted to wide-open farmland, and the sky seemed to grow bigger the further we drove. Every mile brought fresh sights: windmills spinning in the breeze across the plains, shimmering heat waves rising off sunbaked highways, billboards for truck stops and roadside attractions promising mystery and magic.

Dad played classic country on the radio—Johnny Cash, Merle Haggard, Patsy Cline—and when we passed a long stretch of highway, we'd all belt out songs as a family, our voices rising above the rumble of the road. Mom, ever the planner, kept us on track with her notes: where to stop for gas, which towns had decent diners, and where the cleanest rest stops were.

As we moved east, the scenery changed with each passing state. In Colorado, we drove through the shadows of towering mountains, their snow-capped peaks piercing the sky. In Kansas, the world opened up—endless plains stretching so far that the horizon seemed to curve. And then came the Mississippi River, wide and muddy and majestic, shimmering under the sun as we crossed it on a bridge that made the car hum and tremble. America's great artery, flowing slow and strong beneath us, was a sight I'll never forget.

Each evening, as the sky blushed purple and gold, we pulled into roadside campgrounds. We'd pile out of the car, stiff-legged and sun-tired, and get to work. Setting up camp was a ritual. Dad staked the corners of the tent while Ron and I unfolded sleeping bags and helped Mom with the portable stove. Susan and James chased each other between picnic tables, their laughter rising into the twilight air.

Dinner was always something simple—grilled hot dogs, beans in a pot, cornbread from a pan wrapped in foil. We'd sit around the fire, faces lit by its glow, sharing stories and staring up at the stars, which seemed so much brighter out there in the wide-open country. The sounds of the night—crickets, rustling leaves, the distant call of an owl—lulled us to sleep. Some nights we could hear coyotes howling in the dark, a haunting reminder we were far from our California home.

The days passed; each one filled with its own small wonders. We stopped at roadside oddities that seemed plucked from a dream: the world's largest ball of twine, a two-headed snake in a jar, a mysterious gravity-defying "Mystery Spot" that made us laugh and scratch our heads. These moments broke the monotony of the drive and stitched a kind of magic into the fabric of our memories.

And always, there was the anticipation—growing with every state line crossed—of seeing our grandparents in Stonewall. We imagined the look on Grandma's face, the smell of biscuits baking, the swing creaking on the front porch; the dogs running up the dirt path to greet us.

When we arrived, Stonewall Mississippi seemed to rise out of the fields like a memory come alive. It was small and quiet, the kind of place where the time moved slower and everyone waved as you passed by. As we pulled into the gravel driveway of our grandparents' house, we saw them standing there, waiting—Grandpa with his cap in hand, Grandma in her apron, her arms already opening wide.

The house smelled of fried chicken and buttermilk biscuits, and the air was thick with jasmine, honeysuckle, and humidity. We were wrapped in hugs, kissed on the forehead, and ushered inside like we'd never left. The wooden floors creaked just the same, and the sweet tea tasted like sunshine and sugar.

Those days in Stonewall were golden.

We spent hours running barefoot through the woods behind their house, fishing in the nearby creek, and swinging in hammocks hung between trees. In the evenings, we sat on the porch, sipping sweet tea and watching fireflies light up the yard. Family gathered—cousins, aunts, uncles—and the house rang with laughter and stories that stretched long into the night.

We were connected—not just by blood, but by shared experience, by the long road that brought us there, and the love that welcomed us home.

Even now, all these years later, those trips stayed with me. Not just as a memory, but as a *feeling*—of freedom, of family, of the open road and the promise it holds. It was more than a vacation. It was a pilgrimage back to our roots.

During one trip in particular, my father wanted me to come with him alone down to a particular area at the Chickasawhay River about a mile from my grandparent's house. He wanted to tell me stories of his youth. We brought fishing poles to the river and cast the lines into the deep flowing water, then we both lie on our backs along the riverbank. It was easy to see on my father's face how content he was as the sounds of the river and the songs of the birds.

He would tell stories of his early childhood in Mississippi, his friends, and the mischief he would get into. He would often have trails hidden by the house that led down to the river. Running barefoot, he would make his way along the river. As I listen, the stories of Huck Finn come to mind, a young boy, and his adventures along the Mississippi River. Fishing and exploring along an unknown wilderness were his adventures, at least in my father's young mind. He then told me about his secret friend Jeremiah and the tragedy that unfolded. I was in utter shock as I watched the tears flow down my father's face. My father looked at me and asked that I keep this a secret between him and myself.

As the family traveled back across the country to the west coast, I could now see my father in a different way. Deep in his heart, an aching feeling that may never leave.

As successful as life had become on the West Coast, Thomas, now in his early forties, found himself growing increasingly unsettled. On paper, things were good—more than good. The family business in Northern California was thriving. The children were growing up strong and capable, grounded by the stability he and *Betty* had worked so hard to build. Yet, beneath it all, there was a quiet ache that refused to fade, a persistent pull that grew stronger with every passing year.

It was *Mississippi*—his boyhood home, the river, the red clay, the slow lull of southern evenings. He began to feel as though some essential piece of himself had been left behind all those years ago when he first boarded the Navy bus and headed west. He yearned for magnolias, summer heat, and southern stars, even while sitting on their porch, surrounded by large fir trees and the scent of pine in their Burney home.

His childhood friend Jeremiah, whose life was so violently and hastily ended, was frequently in his thoughts. The guilt of surviving—of *leaving*—had never quite let go of him. Their shared dreams of exploring the world together, of making something bigger than the lives they had been born into, still whispered to him in the quiet moments. He felt as though the further he had moved from Mississippi, the further he had drifted from the boy he used to be—and from the promises he had made in silence at Jeremiah's grave.

Not that Thomas didn't love the life he had built. He *did*. He loved Betty. He loved his children deeply. But something in him had fractured under the weight of a life that no longer felt like *his*. Homesickness didn't fully explain it—he was lost. And he knew, deep in his bones, that if he didn't return to Mississippi soon, he might never find his way back to himself.

So, with trembling hands and a heavy heart, Thomas sat down at the kitchen table one evening and told Betty the truth.

"I need to go back," he said. "Not for a visit. Not just to see it again. I need to go back... and *stay*. I need to figure out who I am without all this noise around me."

Betty sat across from him, silent at first, the steam from her tea curling up between them. She didn't cry. She didn't argue. But her eyes filled with a hurt so raw and deep that Thomas couldn't hold her gaze. She understood, on some level—she always had—that Mississippi had never fully let him go. But understanding didn't soften the blow.

"You're choosing a ghost over your family," she said quietly, not in anger, but in sorrow.

Thomas didn't argue. Because, in a way, she was right.

He did not make the decision to leave lightly, nor was it a selfish one. Driven by desperation, it was a last attempt to reclaim the parts of himself he'd buried under decades of duty, grief, and compromise. With shaking hands, he packed his bags, hugged his children with lingering goodbyes, and gave Betty one last kiss on the forehead.

And then he left.

Although not triumphant, he returned to Mississippi out of necessity. As: As his boots touched the warm, familiar earth, something inside him began to loosen. The air was thick with memory. The trees quietly whispered his name. He drove the back roads slowly, windows down, the scent of honeysuckle and river mud curling into the cab of the truck. Stonewall had changed, but it hadn't vanished. The old ghosts were still there—waiting, as if they'd always known he'd come back.

He rented a small house near the edge of town and began rebuilding his life from scratch. He took work fixing fences, working in a hardware store, anything that kept his hands busy and his mind grounded. At night, he sat on the porch and watched the stars emerge one by one, just like he had as a boy, and tried to make peace with the choices that had shaped his life.

The divorce papers were filed quietly. Betty, ever composed, handled the details with dignity and restraint. There were no angry phone calls. No bitter accusations. Just sadness. A slow unraveling of a love that had once held so much promise. They agreed to stay in touch for the children's sake, and they did. But the warmth between them faded into something gentler—like distant friends who had once shared a life.

Thomas's story in Mississippi wasn't one of glory or regret—it was one of reckoning. Of finally facing the past he had run from for too long. Of allowing grief to breathe. At those same banks where he once stood with Jeremiah, he whispered, "I'm sorry," into the wind.

He didn't find all the answers. But he found *honesty*. And in that honesty, a kind of peace.

Thomas's life was not perfect. It was marked by hard decisions and deep sorrow. But courage—the courage to return to his roots, to confront the ghosts he had buried, and to live the rest of his life as fully and truthfully as he could also marked it.

His story reminds us that sometimes the hardest choices are the ones that lead us home—not always to a place, or a person, but to *ourselves*.

Chapter 4

Change

Betty sat behind the counter of the sporting goods store in Burney, the old register quiet beneath her tired hands. Soft afternoon light, filtered through dusty, aged front windows, bathed the store. Outside, the mountains stood tall and indifferent, their peaks dusted with snow, the pines whispering in the wind. Inside, it was still.

Too still.

She stood silently, looking out across the store. Her eyes drifted over the empty aisles and the worn wooden floorboards. Everything felt still. The shelves, once full and busy, now held only a few items, each one meticulously placed but evidently left behind. In one corner, a couple of fishing rods leaned together as if waiting for someone to come back. Nearby, a row of sleeping bags sat folded with care, untouched. A dusty old camp stove sat on a shelf, obviously untouched for weeks. The quiet in the room felt thick, almost heavy, wrapping around her like fog. She found it hard to believe that this space had once echoed with voices, footsteps, and laughter. Now, it was just stillness and the echo of memories.

This place had once been *alive*.

She could still hear the footsteps of little shoes running between the aisles, Susan's laughter, Ron teasing James, Thomas Jr. lugging gear out to a customer's truck. Back then, the store had been more than a business—it had been the heart of their family. A dream carved out of hope and hard work. She and Thomas had built it together from nothing, piece by piece, like the life they thought they'd spend forever sharing.

Now, it felt like a museum of a life that no longer existed.

The sign above the door still bore their name: *Burney Rentals & Sport Shop*. But it was only her name that remained on the paperwork. The *Smith* that had helped start it all was now thousands of miles away, back in Mississippi, chasing a past Betty could never understand and a future that no longer included her.

The divorce had gutted her in ways she hadn't expected—

not just the grief of losing Thomas, but the quiet collapse of their shared identity. She had loved him with everything she had. She had stood by him through war, through hardship, through the winding road of raising five children in the hills of Northern California. But in the end, love wasn't enough to anchor him. He had drifted, and she couldn't follow.

The store was barely hanging on. Foot traffic had slowed to a trickle. The new outdoor mega-store in Redding had swallowed up much of the business, and Betty didn't have the workforce—or the heart—to compete. Every day, her routine involved opening the doors, cleaning the shelves, and balancing the books. She restocked what she could. She smiled at the occasional customer. But most days, the register drawer remained almost untouched, and the only sound in the building was the creak of the old floor when she moved.

She was tired. Bone-deep tired.

It wasn't just the work—it was the weight. The burden of keeping something alive when everything inside you felt like it was slipping away. She was a single mother now, and though the children were growing, they still needed her. Each of them had handled the divorce differently—some with anger, some with silence—but all of them had looked to her for strength she wasn't sure she had left to give.

The bills piled up on the counter behind her. Inventory sheets, tax forms, and hand-written notes she'd left for herself months ago cluttered the back office; all reminders of the never-ending work. Despite that, she pressed on. Because there was no one else. Because giving up felt too much like losing one more piece of herself.

Betty glanced down at her hands, resting over the register—hands that had packed bait and folded tents, that had wiped children's tears and fixed broken zippers, that had signed a divorce decree with steady fingers even as her heart shattered.

She swallowed hard.

Outside, the wind picked up, rustling the trees like an old memory. She closed her eyes for a moment and pictured Thomas as he had once been—standing tall in his Navy blues, or smiling behind the counter with a baby on his hip and sawdust on his boots. She still loved that version of him. But he was gone now—by choice, by need—and she could no longer carry the burden of both his dreams and her own.

Betty opened her eyes and stood, moving slowly through the quiet aisles. She ran her hand along the edge of the counter one last time before reaching up to the pegboard behind her and flipping the "Open" sign to "Closed." Maybe it was time.

Maybe letting go wasn't failure—it was the first step toward rebuilding.

Not what was lost?

But what could still be.

One of the few bright spots during that hard season—the quiet unraveling of the store, the long days of balancing books and keeping the children fed—was Mel. He had started off as just another face in the stream of vendors who stopped by *Burney Rentals and Sport Shop*, back when the place was still humming with energy and Thomas was still by her side. But over the years, especially after Thomas left, Mel had become something more—a steady, unassuming presence in Betty's life when she needed it most.

He wasn't flashy or loud. He didn't offer quick fixes or hollow reassurances. But he had a kind way about him. Betty felt that his patience made her feel like the weight she carried was seen—not judged, just seen.

He'd come in every couple of weeks, clipboard in hand, ready to restock tackle boxes or pick up returned inventory. But their conversations had drifted beyond shop talk. Somewhere in the stillness of those quiet afternoons, Mel started staying longer—leaning on the counter, listening, asking questions that felt deeper than small talk. And Betty, worn thin from carrying the load alone, opened up.

"You're doing the best you can," Mel would say, voice low and warm. He'd firmly rest his elbows on the counter as she let her guard down—just a little—venting her doubts about the store, the finances, the weight of being a single mother to kids who were struggling to make sense of it all.

"It's difficult," he'd add, shaking his head with quiet respect, "but you're stronger than you think."

And somehow, those words meant more than anything she could say back.

Betty appreciated Mel's calm, his way of listening without trying to fix her. But his presence didn't change the hard facts staring back at her every morning. It was failing. The overhead costs are too steep. And more than that—*James* was slipping. Her sweet, sensitive boy had grown withdrawn since the divorce. His grades were falling, his moods swinging recklessly between silence and outbursts. He needed her. Not the version of her that was always behind the counter, always balancing books after dark—but the version who used to sit beside him at the dinner table and genuinely *see* him.

Something had to give.

And so, with a lump in her throat and tears she refused to shed in front of the children, Betty made the hard calls. The rental boats, so full of memories—of sunny weekends on Lake Britton, teaching Susan how to bait a hook, watching Ron leap from the dock while Thomas shouted playful warnings—all of it had to go. She listed the boats for sale. Then the camp trailers, each one bearing the scars and stories of summers past. She walked through each one before selling it off, running her hand along the worn counters, opening the little cabinets, remembering the meals shared inside. Letting go hurt more than she'd expected.

But there was no room for sentiment now.

Mel was there through all of it. He helped her draft listings, called in favors to his network, and made sure she got fair prices for every item. He offered tips, kept things organized, and always seemed to show up precisely when she needed someone to lean on—but never more than she could handle. Never pushing. Never presumptive.

And as the shelves emptied and the back storage room grew bare, a quiet comfort began to settle between them. He started bringing her coffee when he stopped by. She began asking him to stay a little longer. They stretched their conversations from product margins to family stories, childhoods, regrets, and the strange hope that sometimes shows up after everything has been torn apart.

He wasn't Thomas. He didn't try to be. Mel didn't share her history, her kids, or the weight of years spent building a life

from the ground up. But he met her where she was now—in the ashes—and gave her something she didn't realize she'd needed:
Possibility.

One chilly afternoon, with the rain tapping persistently against the windows and the aisles almost cleared out, Mel leaned on the counter, same as always. But this time, he looked at her differently—his expression tender, a little uncertain.

"You ever think about what comes next?" he asked gently. "When the shop's closed for good? I mean—not just what's next for the business, but for *you*."

Betty looked up from the invoice she'd been folding, her fingers still and her breath caught somewhere between her chest and throat.

"I think about it every day," she admitted, her voice scarcely above a whisper. "But I haven't let myself say it out loud."

Mel hesitated, then smiled—quiet and sincere.

"Well," he said, "I've been thinking too. And if you're open to it... maybe we could figure it out together."

The words hung in the air between them—not rushed, not romantic in the grand, sweeping sense—but real. Honest. A question with no pressure, no expectations. Just two people standing in the ruins of what used to be, trying to imagine something new.

And for the first time in a long time, Betty didn't feel like she was standing still.

She felt like maybe—just maybe—life hadn't stopped. It had undeniably *shifted*.

And she was ready to see where it might go next.

"Betty," Mel said one quiet afternoon as they stood side by side in the nearly vacant store, the dust catching in the shafts of light that filtered through the front windows, "why don't you come with me to Oroville? I've got a place there— nothing fancy, but it's quiet. Maybe a fresh start would be good for you and the kids."

His voice was soft but steady, free of pressure, just an open offer—a door she could step through if she chose.

Betty didn't answer right away. She stood there in the hollow silence of what had once been the center of her family's world, her arms folded, her gaze tracing the outlines of the empty shelves and bare pegboards. The walls still held echoes—of Thomas's laughter, the children's footsteps, the buzz of busy summers. The thought of leaving Burney felt like *another ending*, another piece of herself being set aside. She had spent so many years building a life here. Letting go felt like a betrayal.

But deep down, she knew the truth.

The store was gone. The dream was over. And staying meant waking up each morning to ghosts—of a marriage that had unraveled, of children growing up too fast in a home filled with quiet sorrow, of a woman who had once believed she could carry everything on her shoulders and now stood empty-handed.

Betty looked up at Mel then, her eyes searching for hesitation in his face, some flicker of uncertainty that would make her pull back. But all she saw was sincerity. Gentle, patient, real. He wasn't trying to fix her. His offer wasn't a fairy tale. He was offering the possibility. Stability. A new page.

He had stood by her during her lowest moments—never asking for anything, never expecting more than what she could give. And now, here he was again, offering her and her children something she hadn't allowed herself to imagine in a long time:

Hope.

"Alright," she said conclusively, the word quiet, but sure. Her voice trembled slightly, not from doubt—but from release. "Let's go to Oroville."

The move was both liberating and heartbreaking. Betty, James, and Susan packed what they could into borrowed boxes and secondhand suitcases. The rest they left behind—items for donation, memories for the attic, and pieces of the past that no longer fit the future.

Thomas Jr. decided to stay behind, at least for a while. At

eighteen, he was already a man, and he felt responsible for helping prepare the family's old home for sale, ensuring a smooth transition. Betty was proud of him, though her heart ached to drive away without him in the backseat.

As they pulled out of Burney for the last time, the town gradually vanished in the rearview mirror—its familiar trees, the cracked sidewalks, the store with the faded sign. Betty kept her eyes fixed on the road ahead, one hand on the wheel, the other gently brushing James's hair as he dozed beside her.

Oroville was bigger, but quieter. Set against the backdrop of rolling hills and the slow-moving Feather River, it lacked the rugged charm of Burney, but it had a calm rhythm that soothed her spirit. The air was warmer, the nights quieter. It was a place where no one knew her story, where the past didn't walk the streets like a shadow.

Mel had a modest ranch-style house on the edge of town— three bedrooms, a little backyard with wild grass, and a wide front porch where Betty could drink her morning coffee and listen to the birds. It wasn't grand. But it was *theirs*. A blank slate.

The children adjusted gradually. Susan, now in high school, found solace in the new library and gravitated toward a neighbor girl who showed her around the school. James, more sensitive, took longer to settle. He missed the trails behind their old house, missed his brother, missed the way things *used to be*. With unwavering patience, Mel supported him, never replacing Thomas, but consistently providing small gestures of kindness and understanding.

As the weeks turned into months, life began to take root.

Betty found part-time work as a bookkeeper, working for a couple of local businesses and doing income tax work during the start of the year. She and Mel shared dinners on the back patio, music playing gently from the kitchen window, the children's laughter drifting through the house.

It wasn't perfect. There were still days when grief crept in uninvited—moments when Betty would find herself staring at an old photograph, wondering how everything had changed. She still loved Thomas in her own way—not romantically, not anymore, but with the deep ache of someone who had shared too much of their life to ever forget.

But there was something new blooming inside her now—not joy precisely, but peace.

She had left behind a broken past not because she didn't care, but because she ultimately understood that starting over wasn't a failure.

It's courage.

And in Oroville, with Mel beside her, with James and Susan trying to adjust to a new town, Ron was married and working in southern California. Betty finally believed that it wasn't too late to find happiness again. Not the kind she had lost.

But the kind she could build, one quiet day at a time.

James, however, didn't take to the change as easily as Betty and Susan did. The move to Oroville may have offered a fresh start for some, but for James, it only deepened the cracks that had already formed. The divorce had left a wound he didn't have the words to name, and with each mile they had driven away from Burney, away from the only life he had ever known, it was as though he'd lost a piece of himself; he wasn't sure he'd ever get back.

He was just fourteen—too young to understand the complexities of adult choices, yet old enough to feel the full weight of abandonment. He had looked up to his father, even when things were falling apart. And when Thomas had left, James had said little. He hadn't cried. Silence was his response. He had clearly closed off, silently, folding in on himself, like someone bracing for an impact that never came.

Betty had hoped—*prayed*—that the move would offer him a chance to reset. That maybe the clean air, the slower pace, the distance from memories might clear his mind, soften his edges. But the opposite seemed to happen. James grew more distant, more restless. He scarcely spoke at dinner, often retreating to his room or disappearing for hours at a time. His schoolwork, once solid if not stellar, plummeted. Teachers called home, concerned. Notes came back marked with red ink and indifference. His once-bright eyes now carried a guarded, vacant look. As if he was always somewhere else.

Betty noticed him walking home with boys she didn't recognize—older kids, rough around the edges, with cigarettes tucked behind their ears and eyes that tracked everything like they were casing the world for weakness. She would watch from the window, a pit growing in her stomach, every instinct in her body screaming that something wasn't right.

She and Mel tried everything. They invited him to talk. Encouraged him to join family meals, to go fishing, to help around the house. Mel, in his quiet way, tried to connect— to offer James something like guidance, like presence. But James would shrug them off, mumble answers, avoid eye contact. When they suggested counseling, James rolled his eyes, spat out "I'm not crazy," and slammed his bedroom door hard enough to rattle the windows.

"Mom, I'm fine," he would mutter whenever Betty asked how he was doing. But she could see it in his body—how tightly he held himself, how rarely he laughed anymore, how guarded his voice had become. She knew he wasn't fine. She could feel the distance widening every day, like she was watching him drift further out to sea, unable to swim fast enough to bring him back.

Then, one evening just after sunset, the knock came at the door.

Betty froze the moment she saw the uniformed figure

122

through the window—the local sheriff, standing tall with his hat in hand. The air in the house turned cold and still. Her heart thundered in her chest.

"Mrs. Smith," the sheriff said, nodding politely, his tone low and gentle. "I'm here to talk to you about James."

She ushered him in with trembling hands. Mel came in from the back porch and took a seat beside her at the kitchen table, the weight of the moment hanging over them like storm clouds.

The sheriff explained James had been seen hanging around with a group of boys known for stirring up trouble—nothing major yet, but they were *drifting*. Trespassing on private property. Skipping school. Drinking. Breaking into old sheds for a thrill. *So far*, James hadn't been caught doing anything illegal. But it was clear to anyone paying attention that he was skating too close to the edge.

"He's a good kid," the sheriff said, his voice heavy with concern. "But he's hurting. And if someone doesn't reach him soon, I'm afraid we'll be having a much different conversation the next time I'm at your door."

Betty nodded, her fingers digging into the edge of the table. Her throat felt tight; her chest hollow. Even though part of her had known, hearing it out loud broke something open in her. When the sheriff left, the front door clicked shut with a finality that echoed down the hallway.

She sat at the kitchen table, her head in her hands, the quiet of the house pressing in around her. Mel stood nearby, unsure of what to say, wanting to help but knowing some things are beyond fixing, only felt.

How had they gotten here?

She had done everything she could. Had held their family together through heartbreak and upheaval, made the hard choices, pulled them forward through the fog of grief. Despite that, she was losing James. Bit by bit. Day by day. And the truth of it shattered her.

It wasn't just that he was pulling away.

It was that he no longer seemed to believe he could come back.

"Betty," Mel said, his voice little more than a whisper as he placed a steady hand on her shoulder. "We'll get through this. He's hurting, but he's not beyond saving. We just have to figure out how to reach him."

Betty felt a wave of warmth wash over her from his touch, but her response was distant. Her gaze remained on the kitchen table; she stared through the worn wood grain, searching for answers she hadn't yet found. She had tried everything—counselors, school meetings, support groups for single mothers—each path pursued with a fierce hope that maybe, just maybe, this would be the breakthrough. But James remained locked in his silence, his rebellion growing more reckless with each passing week. His pain felt unreachable. Buried behind a wall, she could no longer scale.

She had always believed that if she just loved her children hard enough, they'd come through anything.

Now she wasn't so sure.

Her sense of helplessness deepened like a slow fall. There were moments she'd hear the back door creak open after midnight and breathe a shaky sigh of relief just because

James had made it home alive. But that wasn't living. That was waiting—for something worse. For a knock on the door. For a call in the middle of the night.

And so, with her heart splintering, Betty did the one thing she had avoided for years—the thing she once swore she wouldn't do unless it was undoubtedly necessary.

She called Thomas.

Thomas was living a quiet life in Stonewall, Mississippi, in a small clapboard house tucked beneath the same trees that had shaded his boyhood. He had carved out a modest, solitary existence—worked part time at a hardware store, kept to himself, sometimes joined the old timers at the diner for coffee. He tried not to dwell on the past, though it followed him everywhere—carried in the red clay under his boots, in the river's pull, in the voices of children that weren't his echoing through the streets.

He had told himself the divorce was necessary—that Betty and the kids deserved a man who wasn't half a ghost. And yet, the guilt never left him. Not really. It just settled in like dust on old picture frames. He thought of the children often, especially James, the boy who had once followed him around like a shadow, wide-eyed and curious, always asking questions about tools, nature, the war.

He hadn't heard Betty's voice in over a year, not since a brief, stilted conversation about property paperwork. So, when the phone rang late one evening, he somehow knew there was trouble. His breath caught in his chest. He knew before he picked up that something was wrong.

"Betty?" he whispered.

There was a pause—longer than it should have been—and then her voice came through, shaky, tired, stretched thin.

"Thomas... it's James. He's falling apart."

Thomas said nothing, just listened, his free hand pressed against the counter to steady himself.

"He won't talk. He's angry, distant. Failing in school. The sheriff came by the house. He has done nothing illegal yet, but it's only a matter of time." Her voice cracked, and when she spoke again; it was scarcely more than a breath. "I've tried everything, but I can't reach him. I believe he's carrying more than he knows how to handle. And I don't know what to do anymore."

The words hit Thomas like a gut punch. *He's falling apart.* And unexpectedly, the distance between Mississippi and California felt like a canyon he had foolishly convinced himself could be bridged by letters and birthday cards. He had believed, in some twisted attempt at self-preservation, that leaving had freed them all to grow. But now he saw what had grown in his absence—hurt, confusion, a boy who had once looked at him with trust and now walked the edge of a path he might not come back from. His voice was hoarse when he ultimately replied.

"I'll come to California," he said, the words rolling out before he could question them. "I'll do whatever it takes to help him. Just tell me where to go."

There was silence on the other end, then the quiet sound of Betty's breath—trembling, but full of something else too: relief.

"Thank you, Thomas," she said.

And for the first time in years, they weren't exes on opposite sides of a broken marriage.

They were parents.

And they had a son to save.

Thomas's arrival in Oroville was like a jolt to the heart James didn't know he'd been bracing for. The moment James saw his father step out of that rusty blue pickup—taller than he remembered, more worn, with grayer hair—something him inside suddenly gave way.

It had been many months since he'd last seen his dad. Maybe longer. Long enough that the pain of his absence had hardened into a kind of armor, something James wore every day without realizing it. And now, just like that, Thomas was standing on the gravel driveway, a duffel bag in one hand and the weight of unspoken apologies in the other.

James didn't say a word at first. Just stared. His fists clenched at his sides; his jaw tight. There were too many emotions, all tangled up and screaming to be heard—anger, confusion, resentment, and underneath it all, something more dangerous: hope.

Because even after everything, some part of him still wanted to believe that maybe his father hadn't left *him*—not really. That maybe there was a reason. That maybe, somehow, Thomas had come back to fix what had broken.

But the questions hung thick in the air.
Why now?
Why did you leave?
What do you expect me to feel?

Thomas didn't force anything. He didn't reach for a hug, didn't try to explain himself right away. He clearly offered a soft, "Hey, James," and let the silence do the rest.

Over the next few days, he made himself present, not imposing but *available*. Thomas appreciated that Mel let him stay in a separate guest house on the property. He helped Mel patch a fence in the backyard, offered to cook dinner one night, and asked Betty what she needed without stepping on her space. But most of all, he focused on James.

Not with lectures or demands
 But with time.

He invited James to take a walk with him through the oak lined trails just outside town. At first, James kept his distance, hands in his hoodie pockets, head down. But Thomas didn't push. He walked beside his son, pointing out things they passed—a hawk circling overhead, an old tree with initials carved deep into the bark, a possible fishing hole.

They fished together at the Feather River, casting lines into the slow-moving water in quiet companionship. They said little, but the act of being there—just *being*—spoke louder than words ever could. In the evenings, they'd sit on the porch together, watching the sky bleed orange and pink over the hills, the silence between them progressively softening. It was slow work—the rebuilding of trust. But brick by brick, it started to happen.

And then, one night, as the sun melted into the trees and the cicadas began their nightly hum, James ultimately spoke.

"Why did you leave, Dad?"

He spoke quietly, almost whispering, but every syllable was laced with raw pain. He didn't look at his father, just stared out at the horizon, his arms wrapped tightly around his knees. Thomas took a deep breath. His throat tightened. *This* was the moment—the one he had both feared and prayed for. There were no perfect words. No excuses that would make up for the years lost.

"I thought I was doing what was best for you," he said slowly, his voice thick with regret. "I thought if I left... maybe it would hurt less. Maybe it would be easier for everyone. But I see now... I was wrong. I was wrong to walk away. I should've stayed."

James turned his head somewhat, and the tears welling in his eyes caught the last of the fading light.

"I needed you," he said, holding his voice steady. "I still do." Thomas reached out, firmly, placing a hand on his son's shoulder, the contact warm and grounding.

"I know," he said, his own eyes brimming. "And I'm here now. I'm not going anywhere."

It wasn't a grand moment. There were no soaring speeches or sweeping forgiveness. Just two broken hearts reaching toward each other in the stillness of a California evening. But something shifted in that moment.

The wall cracked.

The ice melted.

And the space between them began to heal.

With Thomas's presence, James slowly climbed out of the darkness that had engulfed him. It wasn't a straight path. There were setbacks—moments of defiance, nights when he still didn't come home until after curfew. But now, when he walked through the door, Thomas was there. When his temper flared, his father didn't yell—he listened. When James failed a test; Thomas helped him study. Thomas's presence and the knowledge that he wasn't alone helped him overcome his feelings of being lost.

James was still figuring it out. But now, he had support, structure, and most of all, *hope*.

For Betty, watching James begin to heal was both a blessing and a quiet ache.

She had done everything in her power to hold their family together—given every ounce of her strength, her patience, her love. And yet, it had been Thomas's return that made the difference.

There were nights she cried alone in her bedroom, not out of bitterness, but out of relief. She would hear laughter on the porch—James and Thomas talking quietly beneath the stars—and feel something loosen in her chest.

It still hurt.
 But she wasn't angry.
 She felt a deep sense of gratitude.

Because her son was coming back to her.

And if it took the return of the man who had once broken her heart to help James find himself again, then so be it. She would choose to heal over pride.

Because that's what mothers do.

Life in Oroville wasn't perfect, but it was better. Betty and Mel continued to build their life together, and though there were still challenges, there was also a sense of peace that had been missing for so long.

As for James, he found his way back to himself, guided by the love of both his parents. And in the end, that was enough.

In the meantime, Thomas Jr. stood at the front window of the house, staring out at the quiet streets of Burney. The morning fog had lifted, revealing the familiar sight of the tall pines that surrounded the property. The air was still, the only sound the occasional chirping of birds as they flitted between branches. This place, once so full of life and activity, now felt like a shell of its former self. The sporting goods store that had been the heart of the family's livelihood for years stood just a few yards away, its doors now locked and its shelves empty. It was strange to see it so still.

After his parents' divorce and the family's decision to move to Oroville, Thomas Jr. had faced a tough choice. His mother, Betty, had asked him to come with them; to help her and Mel start fresh in their new home. But Thomas Jr. felt a sense of responsibility to the house and the property they had left behind. This house, this land—it was part of him. He had grown up here, learning how to fix things alongside his father, spending lazy summer days fishing by the nearby creek, and helping his mother with the store. Memories filled every corner of the property, and the sudden idea of abandoning it felt wrong.

So, when the rest of the family packed up and left for Oroville, Thomas Jr. decided to stay behind, at least until the house sold. He wasn't sure how long that would take—it could be a few months or maybe even longer—but he felt it was his duty to take care of the property, to make sure it stayed in good condition until the right buyer came along. It was a responsibility that weighed profoundly on his shoulders, but it was one he carried with quiet pride.

Staying in Burney felt like closing a chapter of his life, but not without giving it the care and attention it deserved. He knew that selling the house and the land wouldn't be easy for any of them. His mother, in particular, had struggled with the decision to leave. This place had been a refuge for her after the divorce, a place where she had poured her energy into raising the family and running the business after his father left. But there was no denying that. With the store now closed and the family moving on, Burney was no longer their future. It was time to let go.

As Thomas Jr. walked through the now-empty store, he could still picture the days when it had been a hub of activity. Customers coming in to rent boats or buy fishing gear, kids laughing as they picked out bait for their first fishing trips. He remembered the days his father had worked relentlessly, alongside his mother to keep the business running smoothly. Those days seemed like a lifetime ago now; a distant memory he carried with him like an old photograph.

The silence in the store was almost eerie, the once-familiar sound of customers and the constant hum of life replaced by stillness. Thomas Jr. ran his hand along the dusty countertop, remembering the countless hours he had spent there, ringing up customers, stocking shelves, and helping in whatever way he could. In many ways, this place had shaped who he was—learning responsibility, hard work, and the value of family.

Now, all that remained was maintaining the property. Without the daily upkeep of the store, things were simpler. He kept the yard tidy, mowed the lawn, and made sure the house stayed in good condition for potential buyers. The routines became a form of solace for Thomas Jr. in the quiet of Burney. Each task, no matter how small, reminded him of the life they had built here and how much it had meant to their family.

Yet, despite the peace he found in his responsibilities, Thomas Jr. couldn't shake the feeling of loneliness that crept in during the long evenings. The house was empty now, the echoes of his siblings' laughter and his mother's voice long gone. Not that he regretted staying—he still believed he had made the right decision—but he missed his family intensely. He missed the conversations around the dinner table, the sense of belonging that came with being surrounded by those he loved. Oroville wasn't that far away, but it felt like another world.

In the evenings, Thomas Jr. often sat on the porch, looking out at the quiet street, the sky above streaked with the fading colors of sunset. The Burney nights were chilly and bracing, with a subtle scent of pine and earth wafting through the air. It was in these quiet moments that Thomas Jr. felt the weight of time. He was no longer the boy who had run barefoot through these woods, nor the teenager who had helped his father with the heavy lifting in the store. He was a man now, standing at the crossroads of his past and his future, unsure of what lay ahead but determined to honor the life his family had built here.

Thomas Jr. knew that ultimately, the house would sell, and when that day came, he would have to say goodbye to this chapter of his life. The thought of leaving Burney for good filled him with a bittersweet ache. This place had been home for so long that it was hard to imagine a life without it. But he knew that holding on forever wasn't an option. His mother had moved on, his siblings were starting new lives in Oroville, and it was only a matter of time before he would have to do the same.

Still, there was a part of him that wasn't quite ready to let go. The house, the land, the memories—they were all tied to who he was. And though he knew that leaving Burney didn't mean leaving those memories behind, it was hard to separate the two from his mind. This was the place where he had grown up, where he had learned the lessons of life, where he had watched his parents' marriage crumble and his family keep going despite the hardships. It was more than just a house—it was a part of him.

As the weeks turned into months, Thomas Jr. found solace in the routine of caring for the property. He fixed the fence damaged by a storm, repainted the shutters, and revived the garden, neglected since his mother's departure. Each small task reminded him of the time when the house had been full of life, and though he knew it was temporary, it gave him a sense of purpose.

There were days when potential buyers came to look at the house. Thomas Jr. would greet them cordially, showing them around the property, pointing out the features that had once made it a home. He could see the interest in their eyes as they envisioned their own lives here, their own families filling the rooms that had once belonged to his. And while part of him hoped that someone would see the value in the house and make an offer, another part of him felt a pang of sadness each time a buyer expressed serious interest. The day was coming when he would have to leave, but he wasn't sure if he was ready.

In the end, Thomas Jr. knew that his decision to stay in Burney was more than just about taking care of the property—it was about finding closure. Staying behind gave him the time he needed to come to terms with the changes in his family, to process the end of one chapter and prepare to start another. He missed his family, but he also understood that sometimes, staying in one place for a little longer helped you find the strength to move forward.

And when the day came that the house ultimately sold, Thomas Jr. would be ready. Not because he wanted to leave, but because he knew it was time. Time to let go of the past, to allow someone else to create fresh memories in the place that had once been his home. Time to join his family in Oroville, to start the next chapter of his life, knowing that Burney—and the life they had built here—would always be a part of him, no matter where he went.

Chapter 5

Finding the Ranch

The sun was sinking low, casting long streaks of amber and burnt gold across the oak-covered hills as Thomas and James rumbled down a narrow dirt road outside Oroville. Slowly, the truck moved, its tires crunching over gravel and dry leaves, dust curling behind them like a fading memory. The road twisted and rose through the rolling landscape, framed by tangled branches and thick trunks that had stood for generations—quiet witnesses to the passage of time.

They had been driving for over 30 minutes now, winding their way through the foothills toward a ranch Thomas had agreed to help caretake. It was remote, half-forgotten by the world, and that was exactly what he was looking for: a place far enough away from everything that had gone wrong.

But this wasn't just a drive. It was something else entirely.

This initiated something new, a tentative chapter neither expected, yet both desperately required. The air grew cooler as they climbed higher, and through the open windows drifted the faint scent of oak, loam, and early evening dew. Somewhere in the distance, a hawk cried out, circling against the fire-washed sky.

Thomas glanced over at James, who sat hunched in the passenger seat, his arms crossed tightly over his chest. He had said little since they left the edge of town. His face remained impassive, eyes focused on the road ahead, but Thomas sensed his son's thoughts were elsewhere. Maybe back in Oroville. Maybe further still.

The last few months had changed them both. James had fallen into a spiral that neither of them fully understood— skipping school, drifting toward the wrong crowd, carrying anger and sadness too heavy for someone his age. Thomas had seen it from afar and felt it was like a bruise he couldn't reach. He hadn't been there when James needed him most, and now, all he could do was try to show up—every day, calmly, with no promises other than presence.

Thomas tapped his fingers against the wheel, thinking of the ranch ahead. He hadn't met Joe Cook, the owner, just spoken to him once over the phone. The man sounded old and tired, like someone who had long since stopped expecting help. He freely offered the place, providing room and board in exchange for upkeep and caretaking with no inquiries.

It was a strange kind of luck, or maybe fate. Either way, it felt like the last good chance they had.

The road dipped into a shallow ravine and rose again, opening onto a ridge where the oaks thinned out and the view stretched wide: fields gone gold in the dying light, a narrow stream glinting between the shadows, and far off, a modest house and barn tucked at the base of the hills.

Thomas slowed the truck to a crawl.

"There it is," he said softly, more to himself than to James.

James gave a perceptible nod. "Looks... quiet."

Thomas smiled, just a little—more with his eyes than his lips. It wasn't a big grin, but it carried warmth and quiet understanding. "That's the idea," he said softly, his voice calm and steady, as if the meaning behind the words didn't need to be explained. It was simple, but it said everything he needed it to.

For a moment, neither of them spoke. The truck came continued to the top of the drive. The mid-morning sun brightened the landscape, and the oak filled hills around them.

Thomas looked over at his son again. "Are you okay?"

James didn't answer right away. His gaze remained fixed on the house above, the barn behind it, and the land awaiting their decision.

"I don't know," he conclusively said. "But... I want to be."

Thomas nodded. "That's enough for now."

And with that, they continued up the dirt road toward the ranch—toward hard work, quiet mornings, and maybe, if they were lucky, a way to find each other again.

But today was different.

Today, Thomas and James were heading toward something

new, not just driving through the hills. Not just a change of scenery, but the chance at a quieter life, a place where the past might ultimately loosen its grip and healing, could begin in earnest.

Their destination was a twenty-acre ranch tucked deep in the Oroville foothills, a property hidden among the oaks and rolling pastureland. It wasn't flashy. It wasn't polished. But it offered something they both needed: space. Stillness. Reset. Thomas had been in touch with Joe Cook, the owner, a man in his fifties who was looking for caretakers to manage the land while he continued working in the Bay Area. Joe had grown up on the ranch—it had been in his family for generations—but his job had pulled him away, and now the property needed attention. It needed hands. It needed a presence.

For Thomas and James, it was more than a job. It was a lifeline.

As they rounded the final bend in the dirt road, the land unfolded before them like something out of memory: a modest, weathered ranch house with a wraparound porch, its paint faded but holding strong. Two outbuildings stood nearby, one a barn leaning slightly to the left, the other a long shed with corrugated metal roofing. Beyond them stretched a patchwork of pasture and orchard, dotted with ancient oaks whose gnarled branches reached wide over the land. The smell of grass, dust, and distant blossoms hung in the air. It was the kind of place that asked for nothing but effort—and gave quiet peace in return.

Pulling into the gravel turnout, Thomas felt a little less tightness in his chest. It wasn't a dramatic feeling—just a subtle sense that this place might hold something they'd both been missing.

On the porch stood Joe, hand lifted in greeting, his stance easy and open. He wore jeans and a button-up shirt with the sleeves rolled to the elbow, and his face was sun-touched and lined—not worn down, but well-used, like the tools hanging from the walls of the barn.

"Welcome!" Joe called out, his voice carrying across the still air. "Glad you made it."

Joe Cook owned and operated a successful bookstore in the San Francisco Bay Area. He still had a few years before he could retire and sell the bookstore. His plans were to find a good caretaker for the ranch until he could retire and live there permanently.

Thomas stepped out and extended his hand. "Thanks for the opportunity."

Joe shook it strongly, then reached for James's hand as well. "You the strong one?" he asked with a wink. James managed a small smile and nodded.

Introductions came swiftly, easy and informal, and within minutes Joe was leading them across the property. He didn't talk like someone trying to impress—he spoke like someone handing over a legacy, showing them not just where things were, but why they mattered.

"I've spent most of my adult life in the Bay Area," Joe explained as they walked. "But this place? This was my grandfathers. My father's. I'm not ready to move out here full time just yet, but I can't bear to see it fall into disrepair. I need someone who'll treat it like it means something."

As they followed him across the dry, soft earth, James and

Thomas took in the land. The main house, though worn at the edges, had charm: hand-built railings, an enormous stone fireplace, large front window, porch chairs faded from years in the sun. The smaller buildings, evidently in need of some love, sparked quiet ideas—workshops, storage, even guest cabins someday, maybe. A vast expanse of land sloped gently to a line of trees, which hid a small pond whose surface glinted in the evening sun. While parts of the fields were overgrown, they weren't lost—they simply awaited attention.

Thomas looked over at James, whose posture had relaxed slightly. He tucked his hands in his pockets, but his gaze remained alert, taking everything in.

"You think you two can handle it?" Joe asked as they circled back to the porch.

Thomas looked toward his son, then back at Joe. "We're not afraid of work."

Joe nodded with approval. "Good. That's all it takes out here—work and respect. The land will meet you halfway."

As the sun slipped fully behind the ridge and the sky turned a deeper shade of violet, Thomas and James stood beneath the creaking porch beams, feeling something rare and unfamiliar—a sense of possibility.

This wasn't home yet. But it could be.

And that was enough to begin.

In a shaded corner of the property, beneath a stand of tall valley oaks, three horses grazed quietly in a fenced pasture. As they moved with slow, deliberate grace, their coats—one a soft chestnut, the other two dappled gray—gleamed faintly in the late afternoon light. The sound of their steady chewing, the gentle swish of their tails, and the occasional snort of breath filled the air with a quiet rhythm that seemed to mirror the land itself—calm, unhurried, grounded.

Thomas paused, resting his hand on the top rail of the fence, his gaze locked on the animals. A soft smile touched his face, the kind that came from a place buried deep in memory. He hadn't seen horses up close in years, not since his youth at his family's house in Mississippi. Back then, they were more than just animals—they were *companions*, a part of his everyday world. He remembered brushing their coats before dawn, the way their warmth felt against him in the cold, and the long, winding rides through fields just like these.

Seeing them now stirred something inside him—a familiarity, a quiet comfort. But more than that, it sparked a thought: *maybe this is something James needs too.*

He faced his son, a short distance off, arms crossed, intently watching the horses. James said nothing, but the tightness in his shoulders had softened, just slightly. He wasn't smiling, but he wasn't scowling, either.

Thomas could feel the distance between them closing—not through words, but through shared stillness. *Animals had a way of bypassing the noise,* of reaching the parts of us that couldn't always speak for themselves. He imagined James learning to care for them, to muck out stalls, to saddle and ride—not just to keep busy, but to reconnect with something tangible, something real. Something healing.

But it wasn't only the horses that captured James's attention.

As they continued walking along the worn footpath behind

the house, they turned a corner and stepped into a clearing—
and there, nestled in a low patch of sunlight, lay the ranch's
garden. It was a sudden burst of color, unexpected and
striking against the backdrop of faded barns and dry pasture.

Rows of vegetables—kale, tomatoes, squash, beans—
stretched in tidy lines beside clusters of sunflowers,
marigolds, and zinnias, their petals bright and vibrant in the
waning light. The scent of earth and basil, along with the
faint buzz of diligently working bees, filled the air.

James stopped in his tracks.

His arms fell to his sides. He said nothing, but his body
seemed to lean forward as if drawn by the energy radiating
from the garden. The silence between them shifted—not
heavy now, but full. Curious. Open.

Thomas watched his son take it in—the abundance, the order,
the wild beauty at the edges. It was as though the garden
whispered a message only James could hear: *Even here, even
now, things can grow. Even after everything.*

They stood for a long moment, neither of them speaking.

And then, slowly, James crouched near a row of strawberries, gently brushing a leaf with his fingertips.

It was a small gesture.

But it was something.

As the light faded and the shadows stretched long across the pasture, the day drew to a close with dinner on the porch. The three of them—Thomas, James, and Joe—gathered around a weathered table that looked like it had hosted hundreds of meals over the years. The evening air was cool now, tinged with the smell of earth and pine, and the sky above had turned from gold to a deep, peaceful violet.

Joe had prepared a simple meal: roasted chicken, grilled vegetables from the garden, and thick slices of cornbread. It was rustic, hearty, and full of flavor—the kind of meal that didn't need frills to feel nourishing.

They ate quietly at first, the clink of forks against plates and the creak of the old porch wood setting a gentle rhythm. Then, conversation began to unfold—slowly at first, but with a natural ease.

Joe discussed the ranch, his family's history there, and the challenges of combining city living with maintaining it. He talked about the rhythms of the seasons, the quirks of the property, the responsibilities that came with it.

"It's work, no question," he said, his voice steady but warm. "But if you put in the time, the place gives back. There's peace here—if you're willing to slow down long enough to feel it."

Thomas nodded, the words settling into him like seeds on ready soil. Across the table, James listened too—not politely, not out of obligation, but with real attention.

As the sky darkened and the first stars appeared, Joe leaned back in his chair and looked at the two of them.

"If you decide to stay on, this place could be yours to shape. Not just to maintain, but to grow. Whatever it becomes—that's up to you."

Thomas looked out at the dark silhouettes of the land stretching beyond the porch, then over at his son. And in that moment, for the first time in a long while, the future didn't feel like something to fear.

It felt like something they could build. Together.

For James, who had spent the past year drifting through life with no proper direction, the idea of starting over on the ranch was both unnerving and strangely hopeful. It felt like standing at the edge of something unknown—equal parts challenge and possibility. The land was rugged, the work ahead unfamiliar, but there was a pull to it—the kind of work that asked for presence, for purpose. And for a boy who had felt lost in the noise of his own mistakes, that was no small thing.

Still, the road ahead wasn't without its complications. James was still in high school, and the weight of keeping up with assignments, attending classes, and staying on track academically hung in the air like a second full-time job. The ranch, with its endless chores and unpredictable demands, would stretch him thin. But maybe that was exactly what he needed—structure, not in the rigid sense, but in the grounding kind. A rhythm to his days that didn't come from detentions or warnings, but from purposeful movement: mending fences, cleaning stalls, studying late under the porch light.

Thomas, ever watchful, saw it all—the restlessness still flickering behind his son's quiet eyes, the uncertainty, the longing. He understood the tension James carried between the boy he had been and the man he was slowly becoming. And he saw this place, this land, as more than just a second chance. It was a canvas.

Here, tucked away in the golden hills of Oroville, with no distractions but the rustling of oaks and the creak of the barn, there was room for change. For healing. For growing into something stronger. Thomas knew the work would be hard, but growth always came that way—through calloused hands, through early mornings and honest sweat.

Together, they could rebuild the ranch—but more importantly, they could rebuild themselves. And for James, the road ahead wasn't just about finishing school or pulling his weight—it was about learning to stay, to invest, to believe that his future didn't have to look like the past he'd been trying to outrun.

And that, for the first time in a long while, was enough to

make him want to try.

As the days stretched into weeks, the ranch slowly reflected the steady effort of two men learning to rebuild—not just fences and stalls, but themselves. The mornings came early, with the first light of dawn spilling gold across the oak-covered hills, casting long shadows over dew-soaked grass. The ranch, once neglected at the edges, now hummed with quiet purpose.

Thomas and James settled into the rhythm of the land. By six o'clock, the house stirred with life—the gentle creak of floorboards, the low nicker of horses outside, the rich scent of coffee filling the kitchen. It was simple. Predictable. And for James, who had once woken to chaos or nothing at all, that consistency became something sacred.

But before the first boot hit the dirt, James made time for school.

Each morning, he sat at the kitchen table, hunched over his textbooks with a pen in hand and a mug of black coffee cooling beside him. The wood was scarred and nicked from years of use, but it was a perfect desk. With the window cracked open, he could hear the sounds of the ranch coming alive—the flap of wings, the wind rustling the trees, Thomas moving about the barn. It grounded him. The stillness of the early hour gave him clarity he'd never found in a crowded classroom.

The local high school in Oroville had been surprisingly welcoming. The administrators knew his story—not in full detail, but enough. They understood this move to the ranch was more than a change of address. It was a chance. And they gave him room to breathe. He attended part-time in person, supplementing the rest through a flexible independent study program, which allowed him to balance education with the realities of ranch life.

And the ranch demanded a lot.

Every day brought a new task: patching barbed wire fences, hauling feed, clearing brush from the pasture, or rebuilding the garden beds Joe had once tended. Some days, they spent hours in the sun, working side by side without many words. Other days were quiet, slow—just the rhythm of work, the scrape of shovels, the splash of water troughs being filled, and the occasional grunt of effort breaking the still air.

For James, this physical labor was a kind of therapy. He had spent so long drifting, trapped in his own head, tethered to mistakes he didn't know how to fix. But out here, the work was tangible. Clear. When he drove a post into the ground, he could feel it hold. When he mucked a stall, he could see the difference. It didn't lie. It didn't pity. It simply asked for effort—and gave back peace in return.

He'd never say it out loud, but something about the quiet repetition of ranch work soothed him. It gave his restless mind something to do. His afternoons were a balance of sweat and study, sometimes crashing into bed with sore muscles and ink-smudged notes still tucked into his jeans pocket.

It wasn't easy—not by a long shot. There were days he wanted to quit, mornings when the alarm felt like a curse. But still, he kept showing up.

Because for the first time in a long time, James wasn't just surviving—he was growing.

The ranch had become more than a refuge. It had become a classroom, a counselor, a mirror. It taught him patience, focus, and the deep, quiet satisfaction of building something with your own two hands.

And as the land began to bloom beneath their care, so did James—in ways neither he nor Thomas had dared to hope.

Despite the mounting responsibilities that came with life on the ranch, James's grades steadily improved—a quiet but significant shift that didn't go unnoticed. The ranch, with its long days and hard-earned fatigue, had become more than a place to work. It was, in many ways, a sanctuary—a space that stripped away distractions and offered a kind of focus he'd never experienced before.

The rhythm of ranch life—early mornings, daily tasks, and structured evenings—brought a discipline to James's world that no classroom or counselor had ever been able to provide. And within that rhythm, something began to settle inside him. He no longer rushed through assignments or avoided difficult work. He studied with intention, took notes with care, and showed up to his classes—whether in person or remote—with a sense of quiet purpose.

His teachers noticed. The boy who had once been withdrawn

and apathetic was now engaged, thoughtful, even eager at times. Assignments were turned in early. Questions were asked. When one teacher called to check in with Betty, she barely recognized the student being described.

"He's focused, he's trying, he's present," the teacher had said. "Whatever's happening out there... it's working."

James heard the praise through the grapevine, and while he didn't show much emotion on the outside, the words stuck with him. For the first time in years, he felt proud—not just of a grade or a comment, but of the person he was becoming.

Of course, it wasn't easy.

There were days when schoolwork felt impossible—when his back ached from hauling bales of hay, when his hands were blistered from digging postholes, and the idea of opening a textbook felt laughable. There were nights when exhaustion weighed so heavily on his shoulders that he'd fall asleep over his notes, a pencil still tucked between his fingers. But through it all, Thomas was there.

He never pressured James, never hovered, but he was a

constant presence—steady, supportive, and quietly proud. On the hardest days, when frustration boiled to the surface or when James questioned whether the work was worth it, Thomas would pull up a chair beside him at the kitchen table or pass him a mug of coffee in the early hours before chores.

"I know it's tough," he'd say. "But you're doing something most people wouldn't even try. This is what building a life looks like. It's not clean. It's not easy. But it matters."

And James believed him.

Bit by bit, juggling ranch work and school turned into more than just a challenge—it became a way of life that gave James structure, self-respect, and a growing sense of who he was. He was no longer just the kid who had fallen off track. He was a student. A worker. A son trying his best. And with every fence he mended and every assignment he turned in, he carved out a place for himself—not just on the ranch, but in the world beyond it.

It wasn't perfect. But it was real. And for James, that was enough to keep going.

The horses, more than anything else on the ranch, became a quiet refuge for James—a source of solace, strength, and something resembling trust. At first, he approached them cautiously, unsure of himself, unsure if he even belonged in their presence. But horses have a way of sensing emotion, of responding to energy not with judgment but with honesty. And slowly, almost without realizing it, James began to form a bond—especially with a calm, amber-eyed gelding named Buck.

Each morning, before the sun had fully climbed over the hills, James would make his way to the barn, the ground still damp with dew, the ranch hushed in the stillness of dawn. The air was crisp, clean—carrying with it the earthy smell of hay, leather, and the musky warmth of the horses waiting in their stalls. Buck would greet him with a soft whinny and a gentle nudge, as if he knew James needed the ride as much as the horse needed the exercise.

The ritual became second nature: brushing down Buck's coat, checking his hooves, cinching the saddle with practiced care. There was something meditative in the motions—a quiet rhythm that grounded James, easing the noise in his mind before the demands of the day began.

Once mounted, James would guide Buck through the winding trails that crisscrossed the property, following dirt paths beneath ancient oaks and through tall grasses that shimmered gold in the morning light. The views were breathtaking—rolling hills dotted with orchards, the distant Sierra Nevada etched against the sky, and the glint of the Feather River far below, winding through the valley like a silver thread.

Up there, in the quiet hush of the hills, James found something close to freedom.

The ranch, with all its work and responsibilities, could sometimes feel heavy. School still loomed, always reminding him of what he needed to catch up on, who he used to be. But on horseback, the pressure melted away. His body relaxed into the rhythm of Buck's gait; his thoughts became untangled with every mile. Sometimes he would ride for an hour, saying nothing, just listening—to the creak of saddle leather, the sound of hooves on packed earth, the rustle of wind through the trees. Other times, he would speak aloud—not to anyone in particular, but to the hills, the sky, the silence.

Those rides became his sanctuary. A time to reflect, to breathe, to rebuild the parts of himself that had been lost in the chaos of the last few years. He rode not to escape, but to return—to himself, to stillness, to a growing sense of who he was becoming.

And as the days passed, Thomas noticed the change. He saw the way James moved now with a quiet confidence, how he handled the horses with care and focus, how he returned from the hills with dust on his boots and something lighter in his eyes.

He said little about it—just offered a nod now and then, or an extra biscuit with breakfast.

But both of them understood.

In the saddle, James was healing.

And as the land responded to their care, so too did the boy— steady, strong, and learning to trust the trail beneath him again.

Thomas, meanwhile, found his own kind of purpose in the

quiet resurrection of the ranch's aging buildings. Where others might have seen rot, sagging rooflines, and peeling paint, Thomas saw *potential*—the hidden strength of seasoned wood, the resilience in structures built by calloused hands generations ago. With decades of experience in carpentry and construction, he didn't hesitate. Instead, he rolled up his sleeves, brought out his old set of tools, and got to work.

What started as a few simple repairs—like fixing loose boards and straightening old doors—quickly grew into a full restoration project. The smallest building, once filled with dust, broken tools, and forgotten gear, was cleaned out and transformed into a bright, useful workshop. Another outbuilding was turned into a neat and tidy storage shed, with tools hung in order on the walls and shelves built from old wood. Then, after weeks of planning and hard work, Thomas fixed up a third structure—a worn-down shack sitting at the edge of the orchard. He turned it into a warm, welcoming guesthouse, adding a wood-burning stove, a bed frame he built by hand, and windows that looked out over the peaceful hills.

Each nail he drove, each beam he reinforced, was a minor

act of reclamation—not just for the ranch, but for himself. He was building more than rooms; he was rebuilding a life, one board, one breath, one sunrise at a time.

And just as the surrounding structures around them began to stand tall again, so too did the heart of the ranch: the garden.

Unlike the buildings, which Thomas tackled mostly on his own, the garden was a shared space, one where he and James worked side by side, day after day, shoulder to shoulder. They started small—tilling the soil by hand, hauling in compost, turning dry, compacted earth into something soft and ready. It was dirty, sweaty work, but there was something sacred in it, something unspoken in the way they moved together—learning to anticipate each other's pace, sharing quiet jokes, occasionally letting silence speak for them.

They planted in rows—corn, zucchini, bell peppers, tomatoes, onions, and a few herbs for good measure. James took particular pride in the heirloom tomatoes, watching them closely each day, staking the vines with careful hands. Thomas, meanwhile, built raised beds from leftover lumber, shaping them with precision and a craftsman's eye.

And slowly, under the Oroville sun, the garden came alive.

Tall stalks of corn swayed in the wind, tassels catching the late afternoon light like golden flags. Tomato plants swelled with fruit, heavy and warm to the touch, their skins split from the sun. Zucchini vines crept across the soil, their broad leaves sheltering blooms that would soon become dinner. Peppers burst into color, reds and yellows and greens glowing like lanterns among the leaves.

But the real transformation wasn't just in the soil. It was between father and son.

As the garden flourished, so did their connection. They spoke more easily now, trading stories while they worked— memories from Thomas's childhood, questions James had never thought to ask before, quiet moments of shared laughter. Their conversations weren't always deep, but they didn't have to be. The act of working the land together—of planting, watering, harvesting—was its own language.

It was in the garden, with hands in the dirt and sweat on their brows, that the slow mending of their bond took root.

And as they stood one evening at the edge of the garden, looking out over rows of thriving plants glowing orange in the light of a setting sun, Thomas reached over and gently clapped a hand on James's shoulder.

"We built this," he said, voice low and full of meaning.

James didn't answer right away, but he nodded, his eyes scanning the garden—the proof of their effort, of their time, of something growing not just from the ground, but from between them.

In that moment, neither of them felt lost anymore.

They were rooted. Together.

In the quiet rhythm of their new life on the ranch, just as Thomas and James had begun to find their footing, an unexpected shift occurred—one that would deepen their journey in ways they hadn't anticipated. Thomas Jr., the eldest son, who had been living in Burney, reached out one evening with a simple but powerful message: he wanted to come to Oroville to be with family.

The call had caught Thomas off guard. While he had always maintained a strong and respectful bond with his eldest boy, their time together had grown sparsely over the years—a casualty of busy lives, distance, and unspoken emotional gaps. There had never been a falling-out, only the slow, inevitable drift that can happen between grown men who care deeply but don't always know how to show it.

Now, hearing Thomas Jr.'s voice on the line, laced with something like longing, Thomas didn't hesitate.

"Come out here," he said simply. "We've got the space. And there's always work to be done."

A few days later, Thomas Jr. pulled up the gravel drive, the sound of his van crunching over the dirt echoing between the barn and the hills. The sun was low on the horizon, casting everything in that familiar Oroville amber glow. James was stacking firewood by the fence line, and when he saw the van, he froze for a moment—then dropped the last log and jogged over, a cautious smile tugging at the corners of his mouth.

Thomas stepped onto the porch just as his eldest climbed out

170

of the van.

"Hey, Pop," Thomas Jr. called, wiping his hands on his jeans. "Place looks better than I expected."

Thomas smiled as he walked down the steps, his boots landing softly on the worn wooden planks. Without saying a word at first, he pulled his son into a strong, familiar hug—one shaped by years of hard work and love. His hands were rough, his arms steady, and the warmth in the embrace said everything. Then he leaned back slightly, looked his son in the eyes, and said with a grin, "It'll look even better once the three of us are working on it together."

The dynamic shifted—not in a way that unsettled things, but in a way that deepened the foundation they were building. With Thomas Jr. on the ranch, a new energy settled over the land. Where James was still learning, still finding his rhythm, Thomas Jr. arrived with quiet confidence and a strong back, ready to lend a hand without being asked. He had always been the more independent, steady one, more like his father in temperament, and his arrival rounded out the family in a way that felt right—whole, even.

Days took on a new rhythm. The three of them—father and sons—worked side by side, fixing fence lines, reinforcing the barn's frame, clearing the back pasture that had become overgrown with years of neglect. Thomas Jr. took naturally to the horses, often rising before the others to brush them down, mend tack, or ride the perimeter fence with a thoughtful, solitary focus.

And at night, after the sun dipped behind the western ridge and the air turned cool, they would gather around the firepit Thomas had built near the garden. There, with the crackle of wood and the scent of mesquite smoke in the air, they would share beers, pass around plates of food fresh from the land, and talk.

Sometimes it was surface-level—weather, crops, repair plans. But other nights, it went deeper. Stories from their childhood, memories long buried, the kind of slow, patient conversation that only happens when trust has room to grow.

For James, having his older brother there brought something grounding. He had always looked up to Thomas Jr., even if he rarely said it aloud. There was comfort in his brother's presence—a quiet reminder that healing wasn't something he had to do alone.

For Thomas, watching his sons reconnect—and connect with *him*—was more meaningful than he could ever express. He saw his own younger self in both of them, pieces of his history woven into the way they worked, the way they looked at the land, the way they looked at each other. There had been so much pain between them all. So many missed chances. But now, they were building something together— not just a ranch, but a family, stronger and more honest than before.

As the months passed on, the ranch continued to thrive, so did their relationships. The land had become a living thread, stitching together their daily labor and their shared growth. Once quiet observers of the surrounding changes, the horses now responded eagerly to familiar hands. The garden burst with late-summer abundance. Even the once-crumbling barn stood straighter under a fresh coat of paint and the pride of three men who had made it so.

It wasn't always easy. There were disagreements, long days, and moments of exhaustion. But underneath it all was a sense of purpose, something honest and rooted, that kept them coming back to the work—and to each other.

And in that simple, sacred rhythm of building, fixing, planting, and growing, Thomas, Thomas Jr., and James found what they had been missing all along: not just a second chance, but a home worth staying for.

The ranch was more than just a place to live—more than soil and structure, fences and fields. The ranch served as a sanctuary, a living, breathing space where healing occurred naturally and at its own pace. It was a refuge from all they had endured—broken relationships, uncertain futures, and the ache of absence—and it offered, in return, something simple and rare: peace.

Out there, surrounded by the foothills and the low rustle of wind through the oaks, time seemed to move differently. There were no deadlines, no honking horns or city lights— just the slow, steady rhythm of the land and the daily rituals that stitched their lives together. Each day held its own purpose: feeding the animals, repairing what was worn, planting what would grow. The hard work wasn't a burden, it was a kind of meditation—a way to stay grounded, present, engaged.

Mornings began with the soft glow of sunrise, painting the hills in hues of rose and amber. The ranch stirred awake with the low nickers of horses, the creak of barn doors, the clang of feed buckets. Thomas, Thomas Jr., and James had fallen into a rhythm—not just of labor, but of companionship. Each task they completed together, from fixing the irrigation lines to harvesting ripe tomatoes, added another thread to the tapestry of trust they were slowly, patiently rebuilding.

There were moments of quiet reflection—James walking alone with the horses, or Thomas standing beneath the old oak tree near the edge of the property, his hands resting on his hips as he watched the sun rise over the hills. But there were also bursts of laughter, of small victories: the first egg laid by a rescued hen, the satisfaction of a newly repaired fence line, the crisp bite of the season's first apple from a tree they thought wouldn't bloom.

And every evening, as the sun slipped behind the ridge and the sky darkened into a brilliant canopy of stars, they would gather around the firepit near the edge of the garden. The flames crackled softly, casting a warm light on weathered faces and calloused hands. The fire became a ritual, just like the work. It was a place for stories, for teasing, for remembering things, they had forgotten about one another—and for imagining the lives they could still build.

They spoke about the future with hope, not fear. Of what they could do with the ranch, as they still had a couple of years before Joe Cook would return. Of adding livestock, of restoring the back orchard, maybe even expanding the guesthouse. James talked about finishing high school and maybe studying agriculture or starting his own business. Thomas Jr. shared thoughts of bringing others to the ranch someday—kids who, like James once had, needed space and purpose. And Thomas, quietly listening, felt something warm rise in his chest: a sense of legacy, not in name or wealth, but in effort, in resilience, in love.

Sometimes, the conversations would drift into long silences—but they weren't uncomfortable. They were full. Full of what had been rebuilt. Full of what still might be.

And as the fire crackled, and the stars shimmered above them, the men would lean back in their chairs, stretch their tired legs, and breathe in the cool, pine-scented air. The land had changed them—but only because they had allowed it to. They had come to the ranch seeking refuge. What they found was belonging.

And in that space, in that sacred slowness of life under an open sky, they were no longer just recovering from the past.

They were living again. Together.

One of their most cherished rituals, something that became an anchor in the rhythm of ranch life, was the evening ride down to the Feather River. It started simply—just a way to cool off after a long day of work—but soon; it became something more: a sacred routine, a quiet tradition that each of them looked forward to.

As the sun dipped low in the sky, casting golden light through the oak-covered hills, the three men would saddle up—Thomas, Thomas Jr., and James—their horses already alert and eager, as if they too understood where they were headed. The trail to the river wound through rocky gullies, grassy meadows, and tunnels of overhanging branches, the leaves flickering gold and green in the fading light.

The horses knew the path well. Their hooves moved confidently over the earth, pressing soft, crescent-shaped prints into the trail with a rhythmic calm. The steady sound of leather creaking, hooves striking stone, and the occasional snorts of breath became a kind of music—a symphony of movement and silence, blending perfectly with the rustle of the breeze through the trees.

They rarely spoke much during the ride. Words felt unnecessary. Instead, they listened—to the land, to the quiet sounds of nature reclaiming the evening, and to their own thoughts as they loosened from the pressures of the day. It was in those quiet rides that something deeper began to settle between them—a mutual understanding, a bond forged not through grand gestures, but through shared presence.

The Feather River, when they reached it, was a ribbon of cool, clear water winding through the valley, flanked by smooth stones and tall reeds. Eagerly, the horses trotted to the bank, dipping their heads for a drink, their bodies steaming slightly in the cool air after their ride. The men would dismount, stretch their legs, and settle onto flat rocks or patches of grass, boots kicked off, toes sometimes dipped into the cold water.

There, under the open sky and the first flickers of starlight, the outside world faded away. The river's flow seemed to carry their worries downstream—the weight of the past, the uncertainty of the future, the strain of long days—all swept into the current. What remained was stillness. Presence. Peace.

Sometimes they talked. Sometimes they didn't Occasionally, James would skip stones across the river's surface, his face calm in a way it never was anywhere else. Thomas Jr. would pull a flask from his saddlebag, pass it around, and they'd share a drink in quiet solidarity. Thomas, watching his sons by the water, would feel something close to awe—gratitude for moments like this, when everything broken seemed, if only for a little while, whole again.

They would stay until the sky grew dark, and the stars shimmered bright overhead, their reflections dancing in the moving water. Then, with the same unspoken ease, they would rise, gather their things, and mount their horses for the slow, moonlit ride back to the ranch.

Those rides didn't fix everything. Life remained complicated. There were still hard days and silent dinners, moments of doubt, and old wounds that hadn't yet closed. But at the river, in the hush of twilight, they remembered who they were beneath all of it—men connected not just by blood, but by experience, by effort, by the unspoken promise that they were doing the best they could.

And that promise, like the river itself, was steady, flowing, and always waiting at the end of the trail.

The ranch's garden became more than a patch of soil—it became a source of pride, purpose, and quiet celebration. Under the warm California sun, the seeds they had planted in early spring sprouted with an eagerness that mirrored their own transformation. What had once been hard-packed dirt, scattered with weeds and debris, now burst with vibrant rows of life. It was a daily reminder that with patience, effort, and care, even the most neglected things could bloom again.

Each morning, Thomas, Thomas Jr., and James would walk the garden paths with mugs of coffee in hand, inspecting the leaves for pests, the stems for signs of strength, and the soil for moisture. And as the tomatoes ripened into deep red clusters, and the peppers turned from green to brilliant golds and scarlets, they felt not just satisfaction, but a kind of reverence—as though the land itself was answering their commitment with abundance.

The potatoes and squash came in hearty and thick, the herbs fragrant and full, and when they gathered the harvest in baskets, the weight was more than physical. It was symbolic—proof that their hard work, both in the field and in each other, was taking root. Every meal became a celebration, not just of nourishment, but of effort, unity, and survival. Roasted vegetables on the table weren't just food— they were a story, a shared triumph written in soil and sun.

In many ways, the ranch itself mirrored the quiet, steady healing happening within the family. What was once forgotten had been tended to. What had once felt broken was now thriving. The garden was proof of this—growing not only food but trust, connection, and purpose.

Just as they had nurtured the plants, they had also nurtured each other. They'd learned to listen more, to work through disagreements with sweat and silence rather than sharp words. They shared the burden of hard days, and celebrated the smallest victories—a calf born healthy, a fence standing strong after a storm, a perfect tomato plucked from the vine.

The mornings were calm, starting not with rush or stress, but with purpose. Thomas would sit on the porch with a warm cup of coffee in hand, watching the sun slowly rise over the hills. The air smelled of dust, dew, and the fresh promise of a new day. There was no loud noise or urgency—just stillness and the gentle beginning of another day.

As the sun climbed higher, the work began. But it didn't feel like a burden. The long days were steady and peaceful, with each task becoming part of a natural rhythm. It wasn't just about getting things done—it was about being present, finding meaning in each minor job. Every chore, whether big or small, felt like part of something greater. It was all connected—a shared effort, a simple life built with care, patience, and purpose.

Meals were taken together, often by candlelight or the glow of an old kerosene lamp, with dirt still under their nails and laughter between bites. And when the day's labor was done, the peaceful evenings stretched out before them like a blessing—stars wheeling overhead, the hum of crickets rising from the fields, and the warmth of a fire shared in comfortable silence.

It wasn't just a house, a barn, or a stretch of land. The ranch had become something sacred. A place of return. Of belonging. Of becoming.

It had given them all a second chance—not just to start over, but to become more whole, more grounded, more connected to each other and to themselves.

And as the garden grew taller, the fences stronger, and the home warmer, so too did their bonds—woven into the landscape like roots that would not be easily undone. Here, under wide-open skies and the honest weight of work, they had found what they didn't know they were searching for:

Home.

Chapter 6

Shifting Peace

High atop an oak tree-covered hill, the ranch initially felt like a world apart—a sanctuary of tranquility, where the past's noise muted and the present unfurled slowly, like mist. The view stretched for miles, revealing patchwork orchards, weathered barns, and narrow roads that snaked through the hills like forgotten trails. The land breathed, and so did the men who now called it home.

But at the bottom of the hill, where their property line met a sloping curve of a gravel road, something shifted. What had seemed like a backdrop to their peaceful existence took on a presence of its own. It started with the neighbors—a man, his wife, and their grown son—who lived on a ranch just beyond the stand of oaks that marked the edge of the lower pasture. Their house sat in a clearing, set back from the road, its silhouette visible between gaps in the trees, especially in the late afternoon when the sun sank low behind the hills.

At first, the encounters were nothing more than passing moments—curious glances, polite nods, the occasional half-hearted wave exchanged when Thomas, James, or Thomas Jr. drove past in the truck. The neighbors' land seemed peaceful. Fruit trees stood in rows, and a small herd of goats grazed on the hillside. From far away, the place looked a little wild, like something left alone—simple, rough, and untouched.

But it didn't stay that way.

As the weeks went on, the friendly gestures began to change. The waves grew stiffer. The smiles, more reserved. Just beyond the gate, the son, around Thomas Jr.'s age, would stand watching their truck with unreadable eyes. He never waved. Never smiled. Just watched, his posture rigid, his gaze unwavering. It wasn't overt hostility, but it carried something heavy—an edge, a question, a warning.

Thomas noticed first. He said nothing at first, chalking it up to the natural wariness that often came with rural living. People out here valued their privacy, and newcomers—especially ones who took on land that had sat quiet for years—were bound to attract a few sideways glances. But there was something else. Something unspoken in the way the lower neighbor seemed to hold his wife's arm a little too tightly as they stepped onto their porch, or the way the son never looked away until their truck disappeared behind the bend in the road.

The road that wound along the edge of the neighbors' property was part of the route to town. It had always been uneventful. But now, with each drive, the air seemed to thicken, the oak trees casting longer, darker shadows over the gravel as if absorbing the tension that lingered like a fog. Even the horses grew restless near the fence line. Buck, the gelding James rode, would toss his head and snort as they passed by the stretch of land closest to the neighbor's barn, ears flicking nervously toward the house below.

James felt it too. "They always watch," he muttered one afternoon, tightening his grip on the reins as Buck shied sideways. "Like they're waiting for something."

Thomas Jr., more practical by nature, shrugged. "Maybe they're just curious. We've made a lot of changes up here. Could be nothing."

But Thomas remained unconvinced.

It wasn't just the looks or the silence. It was the absence of any real welcome, the quiet friction that hummed beneath the surface of every encounter. A sense of unease started to build. And it had cast a veil of unease over the ranch they had worked so hard to make into a place of peace.

They didn't speak of it often. No accusations, no drama. But each of them, in their own way, began to adjust—locking gates a little earlier, keeping tools closer, watching the woods more carefully at dusk.

And though the ranch above the hill remained beautiful— sun lite, abundant, and full of the life. Tension was increasing—there was now a sense that they were being watched from the shadows below.

Not just seen.

Studied.

And in the stillness of certain evenings, as the last light slipped behind the trees and the wind moved through the oaks with a sound like whispered warnings, they couldn't help but wonder what, exactly, the lower neighbors were waiting for.

James and Thomas Jr., with their long, wind-tossed hair and easygoing manner, carried themselves with a quiet confidence that spoke of a life lived on their own terms. There was a natural rhythm to the way they moved through the world—unhurried, grounded, untethered by convention. Their appearance—sun-darkened skin, worn denim, shirts loose at the collar, hair falling freely past their shoulders—reflected the spirit of the ranch they had helped bring back to life. But not everyone saw it that way.

Each time their dusty old van rumbled down the hill, past the neighboring ranch below, something in the air shifted. What had once been a courteous exchange—nods, small waves, the occasional smile—had withered into something brittle. The lower neighbors, with their unkept hedges, unpainted fences, and rigid posture, had begun to regard them differently.

At first, it was subtle: a wave not returned, a smile held too long without warmth. But soon, those gestures disappeared altogether, replaced by icy stares, stiffened shoulders, and the kind of silence that shouted louder than words ever could.

James and Thomas Jr., usually lighthearted during their drives into town, began to feel the weight of those watchful eyes. Their conversations grew quieter as they neared the bend where the road cut past the lower neighbor's gate. They no longer waved. Instead, they looked straight ahead, the way people do when they feel they've crossed an invisible boundary they didn't know existed.

One afternoon, as the sun hung low behind the trees, casting long shadows across the road, they passed the ranch again. The lower neighbor stood just behind the fence line, arms crossed, gaze locked on the van like a statue carved out of suspicion. James glanced toward him, then quickly looked away.

"He doesn't blink," he muttered, his voice low and uneasy.

Thomas Jr. didn't reply right away. He just tightened his grip on the wheel and pressed his foot harder on the gas.

"They don't like us," James said after a moment, staring out the side window.

"Doesn't matter," Thomas Jr. replied, though the tension in

his jaw said otherwise.

But it mattered. Because with each drive, the space between the two properties began to feel more like a border than a shared road, and the unspoken disapproval grew into something palpable. It wasn't just about appearance or unfamiliar faces anymore—it felt personal, as though their presence on the hill had disturbed something that had long been left untouched.

Even Thomas, ever the quiet observer, noticed. He watched how his sons stiffened when they passed the lower neighbor's land. He saw the way James's confidence seemed to shrink under that silent scrutiny, and how Thomas Jr.'s usual calm hardened into a quiet defiance. They had come here to rebuild, to find peace. But now, an undercurrent of hostility flowed just beneath the surface, threatening to pull them back into the very tension they'd worked so hard to escape.

The lack of reason exacerbated the situation. No one had exchanged words. No incidents. Just a growing sense of rejection, the kind that didn't need to be explained to be understood. They were outsiders, and their long hair, their youth, their way of life—it marked them as different, and different, it seemed, wasn't welcome here.

The once-idyllic road to town now carried the echo of scowls and sidelong glances, of tension thick enough to feel in the bones. Although the ranch atop the hill remained their haven, each return trip from town reminded them that not all neighbors are friendly, and peace isn't always freely given.

Whatever the reason, the message was obvious.

They weren't just being watched—they were being judged.

And judgment, left unchecked, has a way of growing into something darker.

They met attempts to bridge the gap—a wave from the porch, a polite nod from the saddle, a simple "hello" when passing on the road—with cold indifference. Where once there had been cautious acknowledgment, now there was only stone-faced silence, and with each new day, the lower neighbor's displeasure seemed to harden, like a wall gradually rising between the two properties.

Thomas, ever the optimist, had held onto hope for the first few weeks. He believed in the power of kindness, of time. He figured the neighbors just needed to get used to the idea of them living there, maybe see they were working men, respectful of the land and the community. But that hope withered beneath the weight of glares held too long, of driveways crossed in silence, of doors shut a little too vigorously when their truck passed by.

And with it, the atmosphere around the ranch changed.

Now, instead of the gentle rustling of oak leaves, the easy rhythm of boots on soil, and the soft neighing of horses, the place carried something else—a thick, unnamed undercurrent of tension, like a low hum that never stopped. Birdsong still echoed through the trees, but it sounded more distant now. Even the wind seemed to hesitate, curling through the hills with a colder edge.

The source of the lower neighbor's discontent remained a mystery—a silence more oppressive than words could ever be. There had been no direct confrontation, no angry exchange or territorial complaint. Just that watchfulness, always from afar, always just present enough to remind them they were being seen... but not welcomed.

What began as a curiosity from below had grown into resentment, sharp and cutting. And in response, a strange sense of isolation settled over the hilltop ranch. Thomas Jr. grew quieter, his easygoing demeanor giving way to wariness. James started skipping his rides along the southern fence line. Even the dogs had taken to growling low when they wandered too close to the edge of the property that bordered the neighbors' land.

It was as if the peace they had worked so hard to build was being eroded by something intangible, yet deeply felt.

There was no single event to point to. No apparent reason. Just an ever-growing unease that settled in their bones like dust—quiet but suffocating.

The daily drives into town, once filled with casual talk and scenic comfort, now felt like crossing a border. With each pass of the neighboring ranch, the air grew heavier, as if the land itself was trapped by the rift. The trees along the roadside cast longer shadows, and the gate that led to the neighbors' place always seemed somewhat ajar, like a silent dare or a warning.

In those moments, it became clear: they were no longer neighbors sharing a stretch of road—they had become adversaries without ever exchanging a single harsh word.

And in that silence, something darker had grown.

Back on the hill, the ranch still offered beauty—sunrises that painted the sky in soft gold, crickets singing at dusk, and a garden that continued to thrive under their care. But even in those moments of peace, the shadow lingered—a quiet reminder that not all roots beneath the soil grow toward the light.

The sanctuary they had found was no longer untouched. The slow burn of unspoken hostility, not conflict, cracked it. And while the land remained their home, the question hung in the air like smoke from a fire not yet lit:

How long could peace exist in the presence of something so silent... yet so profoundly felt?

The tranquility of the ranch — rebuilt, cherished—was

shattered in an instant. It began with a single glance through the windshield as Thomas Jr. rounded the bend, his van climbing the familiar gravel road past the neighbors' property. But what he saw stopped him cold.

The neighbor's wooden fence, once just a quiet boundary line weathered by sun and wind, had undergone a grotesque transformation.

The boards were tacked with poster paper of rough, dark purple brushstrokes and covered in strange, unsettling symbols and drawings. Though the artwork looked sloppy and rushed, that only made it more disturbing. What was once a plain, weathered fence now looked like something out of a nightmare—or the pages of a madman's notebook.

Figures with long, tangled hair, drawn in quick, jagged lines, stood out across the boards. Their bodies were caricatures, barely human, but their hair—the shape, the movement, the volume—was unmistakable. They bore a distorted resemblance to James and Thomas Jr., their faces — twisted into hollow-eyed, sneering ghouls, mouths frozen in silent screams. One drawing showed a truck eerily similar to Thomas's, shrouded in crude, shadowy outlines, with jagged

195

black shapes looming over it like specters.

But it was the guns that caused their hearts to tighten in fear. Crude drawings of rifles and scopes were carefully aimed at sketches of the family. Red crosshairs were marked on their heads and chests, sending a clear and threatening message. It was a chilling image—one that didn't just hint at violence, but suggested someone had been watching them closely and targeting them on purpose.

Some figures were distorted and twisted, their bodies stretched and swollen in unnatural ways. They were drawn in sexual poses, some paired with horses, their limbs bent at odd angles that made the scene hard to look at. There was something wild, animal-like, and deeply unsettling about the images. Their faces showed intense emotion—whether it was pain or pleasure, it was hard to tell, and that uncertainty made it even more disturbing.

There was no direct message. The intent was obvious. This was a threat, a statement of domination, of mockery, of something unhinged and unsettlingly personal.

From that day on, every drive past the neighbor's ranch

became an ordeal.

The familiar road that had once offered a peaceful route into town now felt like a gauntlet, a corridor lined with hostile sentinels, each painted plank a silent scream, a hateful whisper. The drawings, with their lurching proportions and haunting eyes, seemed to shift with the light, to follow the truck as it passed, like some obscene chorus of watchers who refused to blink.

James grew quiet, his fingers gripping the door handle as they passed, his eyes fixed straight ahead. Thomas Jr., normally unshakable, began keeping a tire iron beneath the seat, just in case. And Thomas, ever the one to seek reason over reaction, found himself waking at night with a dry mouth, listening for sounds in the distance—a branch snapping, a gate creaking, the engine of a vehicle that didn't belong.

The sanctuary they had built now bore the marks of intrusion. The safety they had felt was gone, replaced by a silent, simmering dread.

And perhaps most disturbing of all, they knew they couldn't

go to the authorities with drawings. No one had crossed a legal line. One could write off the images, however vile, as eccentricity, artistic freedom, or a matter of property rights. There were no names scrawled, no explicit threats—only implication, and the terrible power of suggestion.

But the family knew the truth.

These weren't just drawings.

They were warnings.

Signals from the bottom of the hill, where something broken festered in silence and watched with eyes that had given up blinking.

The sense of danger grew stronger every day, like a fever that wouldn't go away. At first, the symbols on the fence looked like simple, crude warnings. But over time, they became more detailed—more disturbing. It felt like whoever was behind them had grown bolder and more intentional. The figures turned more twisted, their eyes sharper, their movements more unsettling. The purples and blacks grew darker, layered so thickly they seemed to shift or move if you looked at them too fast.

The fence, once a simple line between properties, now felt like a barrier in a war zone—a wall. erected not just out of wood and paint, but out of malice. It had become a grotesque gallery of psychological warfare, broadcasting a message only the three men at the top of the hill could hear. Every image seemed tailored to their lives, their appearances, their fears.

Despite that, they had no answers.

They considered going down to talk to the neighbors, to confront them—but something about the silence that hung at the base of the hill, thick and still like a held breath, made the thought unthinkable. The neighbors never came up. They never spoke. They remained in their house, behind their fence, hidden in shadows, and let the images speak for them.

And speak they did.

A sense of violation crept over the land, as if the air itself had changed. The once-inviting hills, golden and open, now felt tight and watchful. The trees no longer whispered with the wind, but murmured warnings only the heart could understand. Even the sunlight, which used to bathe the ranch in a warm, forgiving glow, now seemed colder, its touch unable to pierce the shadows that gathered in the corners of the property.

Fear crept into every space—under the eaves, across the barn rafters, into the quiet corners of the garden. The ranch, which had once offered healing and sanctuary, now seemed to pull inward, protective and braced for something unseen. The horses, once calm and curious, acted skittish near the southern fence line. They tossed their heads, pawed the ground, and refused to cross certain spots. Whenever James led Buck past the road, the gelding would shudder and shift. Across the property line, the signs hanging on the fence with purple and black smears layering into warped images that seemed to move when glanced at too quickly.

Whatever it was beyond the fence, they felt it too.

Inside the house, the atmosphere became strained. Thomas, who had always been a grounding presence, now sat longer in silence, his cup of coffee cooling in his hand, eyes drawn toward the tree line. He found himself checking the locks more often, inspecting the barn at night with a flashlight, his other hand always holding a bat.

James, once full of extra energy and optimism, had grown withdrawn. He no longer rode alone, and his studies suffered. His gaze often drifted toward the hills, as though he expected something—or someone—to appear.

And Thomas Jr., whose strength had always steadied the family, walked the perimeter of the property at dusk. He said it was just for peace of mind, but the way his jaw clenched and his eyes never stopped scanning the trees said otherwise.

The tension had reached a fever pitch, a steady pressure that coiled tighter with each passing day. They spoke little of it now. What could they say? They were being hunted—but not by bullets or fists. By silence. Through symbols. A presence, though unseen, constantly affected them.

And though the ranch still stood, and the house still held them, it no longer felt like freedom.

It felt like a cage.

A beautiful, hand-built prison whose walls were made not of wood, but of paranoia, confusion, and the invisible grip of fear. Their sanctuary had become their siege grounds. And as another morning dawned over the oak-covered hill, the only certainty they had left was this:

Whatever was coming next… it was already on its way.

Faced with the growing threat, there came a moment of reckoning—an undeniable truth that settled into the bones of the ranch and refused to be ignored. The silence, the watching, the grotesque drawings—they had all pointed toward something darker, something long coiled in shadow. Now, that darkness had stepped into the light.

Only one option remained: they had to confront it.

But as they made preparations—checking the gate locks, walking the perimeter more frequently—the unease that had lingered in the background now surged into the foreground. Every creak in the night, every snap of a branch outside the window felt loaded with intent. The sanctuary they had fought so hard to create—the sweat-earned peace, the fragile trust between father and sons, the hope planted alongside rows of tomatoes and corn—felt like it was unraveling.

And then came the escalation.

What had begun as cryptic, unsettling artwork now became undeniable hate.

The neighbor's fence, once an eerie canvas of strange symbols and disturbing figures, now screamed with open, venomous hostility. Swastikas, drawn in thick, unbroken lines, appeared between the older images—painted boldly in red and black, their geometry unmistakable and chilling. There were no longer questions of interpretation. This was a declaration. A warning. A provocation.

Other markings followed the swastikas crosses, and runes scrawled in jagged patterns across the boards. The brush partially hid some markings; others, positioned at eye level, seemed designed to be seen, to haunt. The gun imagery multiplied, now more detailed, more menacing. Muzzles aimed toward the hill. Figures resembling Thomas and his sons sketched in target silhouettes. One plank bore a crude depiction of a burning house. It was undeniably *their* house.

The air around the ranch thickened with dread.

Each drive past the neighbor's property became a trial of the nerves—a psychological gauntlet, where hatred stared out from wood and wire, daring them to look away. But they couldn't. The fence had become a wall of violence dressed in symbols of white supremacy and hate, its message no longer vague but blunt and brutal.

On their porch, rifles in hand, the neighbors would watch Thomas, Thomas Jr. and James drive by.

The once unassuming boundary now glared, each swastika an eye watching them with malevolent amusement and feeding off their fear. The fence was not just a canvas—it had become a weapon.

And it was working.

Thomas, who had once found solace in the rhythm of soil and hammer, now moved like a man waiting for something to strike. His sleep was shallow, broken by the howls of distant coyotes or the sound of tires on gravel. James, his youthful optimism cracked, began avoiding the garden, refusing to go near the road at all. Thomas Jr. grew quiet, withdrawn, more watchful—always scanning, always bracing.

Something infiltrated their sanctuary—not physically, but spiritually. The hate didn't have to cross the property line to pollute the land. It hung in the air, in the trees, in the spaces between them. It made every sunset feel more like a drawing of a curtain than a promise of rest. Even the animals sensed it. The horses became jittery, their ears flat when passing the lower pasture. The dogs barked at shadows that weren't there, pacing the fence at night with their hackles raised.

Inside the house, the family was still united—but strained. The pressure of unspoken fear bore down on every interaction. Conversations were clipped, heavy with what wasn't said. Every plan for the future felt tentative, every laugh, when it came, rapidly swallowed.

And yet, despite the fear, despite the venom etched into every plank of that cursed fence, there was something else beginning to stir—a quiet resolve.

This was not just about property anymore. Not about land. It had become a moral battleground, a fight for dignity, for identity, for the right to live in peace without fear.

The symbols of hate had poisoned their soil, yes—but they had also revealed something vital:

One must defend that peace when threatened—not just with words or fences, but with courage, truth, and unshakable will.

Attempts to rationalize the neighbor's actions—those grotesque symbols and messages of hate—became a futile exercise in the face of something so profoundly irrational. The swastikas, the gun imagery, the twisted caricatures, all sat rotting on the fence like open wounds carved into the land, festering in plain sight. There was no logic to it, no reasonable grievance behind it, only the heavy silence of ignorance and the suffocating stench of intolerance.

Thomas had always believed that understanding bred resolution—that if he could make sense of it, find some thread of humanity in the madness, there might be a way forward. But the symbols on the fence were not born of misunderstanding—they were born of hate, raw and deliberate. The intent was clear, even if the minds behind it remained in the shadows.

As fear began took root in the ranch's soil, so too did isolation. The ranch, once a sanctuary filled with the warm, earthy rhythm of daily life, now felt like a fortress under siege. Isolation grew as fear took root on the ranch. They had once viewed themselves as part of the larger landscape—connected to the land, animals, and their hoped-for neighbors—but now felt cut off, as if someone had lifted the ranch from the valley and cast it adrift in a sea of suspicion and dread.

Every window felt like an eye. Every sound beyond the tree line was a question. And every trip down the driveway became a calculated act—eyes scanning the horizon, fingers resting near the latch of a gate or the edge of a rifle.

Faced with this creeping threat, Thomas, James, Thomas Jr. found themselves cornered by a choice that none of them had ever wanted to make: live in fear, or confront it.

And so, reluctantly, they armed themselves.

The rifles, shotguns, and revolvers—once symbols of utility

and rural independence—took on a new meaning. They were no longer just tools for hunting or protection against coyotes. They became symbols of resistance, of a family's quiet vow not to be driven from the land they had poured their souls into.

They didn't make the decision in anger. It wasn't a call to arms in the traditional sense. It was a last resort—the drawing of a line in the sand. It wasn't a cry of violence, but a silent prayer for peace that they might never receive unless they guarded it.

Now saddled with a rifle slung across his back, James, once carefree and unburdened, dulled his youthful innocence with the constant pressure of alertness. The sound of hooves on dry leaves no longer brought peace, but tension—his eyes always drifting toward the southern ridge, where the fence met forest, and danger might linger unseen.

Thomas Jr., who had always been the quiet protector, took it upon himself to clean the weapons every evening, inspecting them by lamplight at the kitchen table. His movements were steady, precise—but the set of his jaw, the tightness around his eyes, betrayed the storm beneath the surface.

Thomas, the center of their fragile peace, felt the weight of this choice more than anyone. He had not come to the ranch to fight. He had come to rebuild. And yet, here he was, loading shells into a rifle, feeling the ache in his hands and wondering what kind of world had made this necessary. He felt heavy with sorrow, not for what they had done—but for what they might one day be forced to do.

Even driving into town, they concealed weapons beneath jackets and in glove boxes—a grim reminder that hatred would not rest or yield to reason. They carried the weapons as part of their daily rhythm, a burden borne not from desire, but from sheer necessity. A quiet, terrible responsibility.

That promise of new beginnings, healing, and simplicity— the ranch—had become a battlefield in waiting. Despite everything, the garden still grew. The horses still grazed. But underneath it all, a tension crackled, dry and brittle, like autumn grass waiting for a spark.

And yet, even in the face of that growing darkness, they endured. They did not run. They did not cower. They stood, weapons not raised but ready, shoulders squared against the tide of hate that had crept up the hill.

As they moved about the ranch, the presence of the guns was felt in every motion—a shield and a burden all at once. Where once a belt or a rope had hung from their hips, now there were holsters. The metal pressed against their sides, a silent companion that offered reassurance in one breath and a haunting weight in the next. It was safety, but it was also a constant reminder: danger lived just beyond the tree line, perhaps even closer.

The firearms, once symbols of rural independence or self-reliance, had become something far more complicated—the physical embodiment of fear they had been forced to carry. They were tools, yes, but also symbols. A line in the sand. A whispered warning: We will not be easy prey.

Even the most mundane tasks—checking the garden, fetching water from the trough, fixing a fencepost—were now acts of calculated awareness. Every rustle in the underbrush, every snap of a twig: very shift in the wind, became a potential threat. What had once been the soothing sounds of country life now carried tension, each noise turning their heads, their eyes scanning for movement.

Their refuge, the ranch, which was once filled with the gentle rhythm of animal calls and breeze-swept grass, was now a landscape of heightened alertness. The rolling hills, where they had once ridden freely, now looked like high ground to be held. The oak groves, where they had picnicked and repaired saddles under the shade, now seemed like potential hiding spots for unseen eyes.

Yet despite the anxiety that seeped into every waking moment, despite the nights when sleep came slow and shallow, they did not give in to despair.

Thomas, with the weight of age and wisdom, had seen hardship before. He'd fought through war, through loss, through loneliness—and he wasn't about to let hate chase him from the land he'd finally found peace with his sons. Thomas Jr., steady and resilient, carried the burden with a kind of silent grace. He had become a sentinel, keeping watch not just over the land, but over his father and brother. And James, still so young, but hardened now by all that had unfolded, had grown into a fierce protector in his own right—his resolve forged not in rage, but in love.

They pressed on, not out of pride, but out of principle.

Every morning, they saddled their horses and made their rounds, rifles slung across their backs, scanning the horizon with eyes that had grown sharper from necessity. The hoofbeats echoed in the stillness. Not as noise, but as a declaration: *We are still here. We are not hiding.*

And in the truck, as they drove the winding roads toward town—passing that cursed fence, its grotesque imagery now seared into memory—they no longer looked away. They looked forward. Eyes forward. Shoulders squared. Hands near the grip, but not trembling. Their presence was their answer.

It would've been easier to leave. To pack up, disappear, find quieter soil. But they had understood something vital—that land is not just dirt and trees and sky. A memory. It's home. It's a stand against the dark when the world turns its back.

And so, even as the specter of confrontation loomed, even as the hate from below crept closer with each passing day, they refused to cower. They drew their strength from the earth they walked, from the sweat they'd poured into it, and from the bond between them—father and sons—stronger now than it had ever been.

The rifles they carried weren't for show. And they weren't for vengeance. They were for survival. For protection. For the principle that no one should terrorize a man in his own home.

As the days stretched on and the tension grew heavier, they rode, they worked, they stood tall—not because they weren't afraid, but because they refused to live in fear.

And that, in the face of everything, was its own kind of courage.

One particular day, as Thomas's car rolled through the familiar streets of Oroville, the late afternoon sun cast long, golden shadows across the pavement. It was the kind of light that softened the edges of the world, and as he passed the worn brick storefronts and sleepy intersections of town, his mind drifted—to Jeremiah.

It happened often these days, especially when he was alone. Jeremiah's memory hovered at the edge of consciousness, not a ghost that haunted, but one that accompanied. A quiet presence in the corners of his heart. Jeremiah had been more than a friend—he had been a brother in every way but blood.

In the small Mississippi town where they'd grown up, their bond had defied the brutal lines drawn by a divided world. They'd fished together when the world told them they shouldn't. They'd laughed when laughter wasn't safe. And when the Klan took Jeremiah, it carved something out of Thomas that had never quite healed.

He turned off the main road, his tires crunching over gravel as he neared the Feather River. The water shimmered in the afternoon light, winding its way through the land with an effortless grace that always calmed him. But today, the river carried a heavier pull.

That's when he saw him—an older black man, sitting near the riverbank, a fishing pole resting between his knees, a small tackle box at his side. His hat shaded his face, and the sun warmed his shoulders as he sat motionless, watching the water with the quiet reverence of someone who had fished a thousand times before.

Something stirred in Thomas's chest. He pulled over without quite knowing why; the moment swelling with a strange mix of memory and instinct. He stepped out of the car, the air thick with the scent of water and wild grass, and walked toward the man as if drawn by a current he couldn't resist. "Afternoon," Thomas mumbled.

The man looked up. Years had weathered his face, carving it deeply, but his eyes remained sharp and kind. He nodded. "Afternoon," he replied, his voice low and even. "Fine day for fishing."

Thomas smiled, feeling a weight lift from his chest. "That it is."

Before long, they were side by side on the bank, two men brought together by water and memory, casting lines into the slow-moving current. Their conversation unfolded naturally, carried by the rhythm of the river, the whisper of a breeze through the reeds, the occasional flicker of sunlight off a fish's back.

They spoke of tackle and bait, of stubborn catfish and elusive trout, of the quiet satisfaction in waiting for a bite. But soon, the stories dug deeper, casting back through time.

Thomas spoke of Jeremiah, his voice softening as he described the boy with the crooked smile and endless curiosity. The friend who could make an afternoon feel like a lifetime. He recounted the days they'd spent along the Mississippi riverbanks, barefoot and laughing, swapping stories, ignoring the stares and whispers from people who didn't understand their bond.

"He was the best damn fisherman I ever knew," Thomas said, staring into the water. "Didn't matter if the fish were biting or not. He'd make you feel like they were. And somehow, being near the water with him... it just made things feel right."

The man beside him nodded, his gaze never leaving the river. "Sounds like he was a good one. The good ones... they stay with you. Even after."

Thomas nodded. "Yeah. They do."

There was silence then—not the awkward kind, but the kind that settles like a blanket between people who understand something words can't quite reach. The water lapped at the shore, and the rods remained still, but neither man cared whether or not they caught anything.

They weren't there for the fish.

They were there for the quiet, for the connection, for the echoes of someone lost and the comfort of someone found.

And the sun cast a warm, amber glow across the water, Thomas felt a stillness he hadn't known in years. For the first time in a long while, he felt Jeremiah was close—not just in memory, but in spirit.

He glanced over at the man, who had yet to offer his name. Perhaps it was unimportant. Maybe it wasn't about names.

It may have been about two men on a riverbank, sharing stories and silence, casting lines, and remembering their shared humanity.

But as the conversation unfolded—two men swapping stories beneath the wide California sky, their laughter rising in soft ripples over the murmur of the river—a shadow crept across the light.

A low, familiar rumble of tires on gravel broke the peaceful rhythm. Thomas turned slightly, catching the sound, but not the source, and thought nothing of it. But the man behind the wheel knew exactly what he was seeing. From the bend in the road, just above the banks of the Feather River, the lower neighbor slowed his car to a crawl.

His eyes locked onto the scene—Thomas, a white man, seated beside a black man, the two of them smiling, engaged in simple conversation, their fishing rods resting between them like old friends in communion.

The lower neighbor's face twisted.

What Thomas saw as a beautiful human connection, the lower neighbor saw as betrayal.

To the man who lived just beyond the oak-covered ridge, whose fence now bore the symbols of hate and a mind consumed by bitterness, this moment was an offense. His world was one of boundaries—drawn in race, in blood, in lineage. And in that moment, the sight of Thomas breaking those boundaries lit a fuse in the neighbor's chest. A storm of rage rose behind his eyes, a wild, frothing anger that had no words—only fire.

The car crept past, slow enough for Thomas's companion to notice the way the neighbor stared—not with curiosity, but with pure venom. The black man's posture shifted, just a little. His hand hovered near his tackle box. Not afraid. Not flinching. But aware.

"Friend of yours?" he asked calmly, without looking.

Thomas glanced toward the car's rear window as it disappeared around the bend. "Neighbor," he replied, brushing the word off with a sigh. "Sort of."

The man nodded. "Doesn't look like he much enjoyed seeing us here."

Thomas let out a dry breath, not quite a laugh. "Probably not." He looked back at the river, his eyes following the slow pull of the current. "But I'm not about to let that man decide who I sit besides, or who I share a story with."

For a moment, neither of them spoke. The river whispered, the breeze rustled the tall reeds along the bank, and the world tried to return to stillness. But that moment—that flicker of hatred from the road above—lingered like a noxious vapor, curling around the edges of their peace.

Thomas didn't know the full extent of the neighbor's fury. He hadn't seen the white-knuckled grip on the steering wheel, hadn't heard the growl of the engine revving as it disappeared into the hills. He couldn't yet know how that single image—of unity—had fractured something irreparable in the neighbor's mind.

But he felt the tension. Felt the way the air had changed. How the river no longer sounded so distant from the real world.

And yet—he stayed.

Thomas didn't stand. He didn't apologize. He didn't retreat.

Instead, he leaned forward, tugged lightly on his line, and said, "You ever fish the Mississippi? My buddy and I used to swear the catfish down there were smarter than most people."

The older man smiled. "I've fished it once or twice. Those river cats don't just bite—they fight."

Thomas chuckled. "Good. That means we'd get along."

And just like that, the poison in the air cleared, burned away not by confrontation, but by something stronger—understanding.

Because even as hatred prowled just beyond the bend, Thomas had chosen his ground. He had chosen to remain beside the man, not out of rebellion, but out of principle. Out of memory. Out of love—for Jeremiah, for decency, because connection was stronger than division.

As the sun dipped lower, casting golden light across the rippling water, the riverbank once again felt sacred. Not untouched—but redeemed.

And Thomas, sitting shoulder to shoulder with a stranger who now felt like a friend, knew that in the quiet defiance of compassion, he had already won a battle the lower neighbor could never understand.

Thomas smiled as he drove back to the ranch, thinking about the enjoyable time he'd spent with his new friend by the river.

As darkness descended upon the ranch, the quiet hum of evening gave way to something unnatural—a vile, orchestrated intrusion that shattered the stillness. It began with a low hum rising from the valley, faint at first, like the stirring of some malevolent presence. Then, abruptly, the sound swelled, rolling up the hill in a tidal wave of distortion and dread.

Nazi marching music, blaring from a powerful loudspeaker, tore through the calm night air, its grotesque rhythms echoing off the oaks and hillsides. The harsh, authoritarian drums, the cold, prideful brass, and the chilling cadence of boots on pavement reverberated across the land like a curse. Thomas, Thomas Jr., and James froze, the moment slamming into them like a physical blow. The sound wasn't just loud—it was surgical, targeted. It was aimed directly at them, a weapon of psychological warfare.

The neighbor—emboldened, enraged, and unhinged—had crossed into full-blown terrorism. The choice of music wasn't random. It was deliberate. A reminder. A declaration. This is who I am. And this is what I want you to fear.

From dusk until the early hours of morning, the symphony

of hate continued, a grotesque loop of wartime anthems, Hitler's voice barking through the static, and pounding drums that seemed to march up their driveway, step by step, even though no one was there.

The sound shook the hills, making the oaks tremble like living things caught in a storm. In the pasture, the horses bucked against the fence in fright. The dogs howled and pawed at the door. And inside the ranch house, Thomas and his sons sat in the dark, hearts pounding, nerves frayed to the point of snapping.

And then came the gunfire.

Within a week of the first loud speaker assault, the lower neighbor's harassment escalated. Shots cracked through the night, from somewhere from the lower edge of the ranch house—not aimed, not random, but performed. A spectacle of dominance. The bullets weren't close enough to hit the house, but they sang through the trees, sharp and terrifying, a promise written in fire and echo: *I can reach you if I want to.*

The first night, Thomas dove for the light switch, plunging

the house into darkness, pulling James and Thomas Jr. to the floor as the reports cracked across the valley. "Stay low," he whispered, voice trembling. "Don't move."

The second night, they didn't even wait for the shots. As soon as the sun dipped below the hills, the lights went dark. Curtains were drawn. Phones were gripped with white-knuckled hands. Each night followed the same rhythm: noise, panic, silence, dread.

And every night, they called the police.

Each time, their voices cracked with desperation. Thomas begged them to come quickly. James, shaken and furious, gave names, described the fence, the music, the gunfire. Thomas Jr. stood at the window, watching, waiting, his hand on his weapon, heart thudding with a rhythm that no one should ever get used to.

But the police did not act right away.

They came, eventually—hours too late, long after the music had stopped and the air had gone still. They parked at the edge of the lower neighbor's property, lights flashing briefly in the dark, had a word or two behind closed doors—and then drove away.

And nothing changed.

Each time Thomas asked why, he got the same reply: "We can't arrest him unless we witness it ourselves."

Witness it? he thought. *We're living it.*

Night after night, their sanctuary became a prison—the hills that once gave them peace now echoing with violence and cowardice. The garden remained untouched, but its beauty felt mocking. Although the horses still grazed, they did so nervously. The land hadn't changed—but everything on it had.

In the silence between gunshots and official indifference, fear made its home in the walls. It curled in the corners, whispered in the shadows, slipped beneath the doors with the chill of midnight air.

James stopped sleeping. He sat by the fireplace in the dark, cradling his rifle like a child might cling to a blanket.

Thomas Jr. paced. Outside. Inside. Restless, twitching at every crack of the branches. And Thomas, who had once been the foundation, the rock upon which the ranch had been rebuilt, felt something he hasn't felt since the war.

Helpless.

There were no headlines. No news reports. No public outrage. Just a family huddled in the dark, hoping the next bullet wouldn't be for them.

Despite that, through it all, they endured.

Because leaving wasn't an option. Giving in would have meant letting hate win. Because they had built something here—something real—and they would not surrender it to madness.

But the truth was clear:

They were no longer just defending their home.

They were surviving a siege.

Chapter 7

Origins of Darkness

The Nazi movement that darkened the twentieth century grew from the ruins of World War I. Defeated and humiliated, Germany signed the Treaty of Versailles in 1919. The accord blamed Germany for the war, stripped away its colonies, restricted its army, and saddled it with crushing reparations. Inflation soared, jobs disappeared, and by the early 1920s ordinary Germans needed wheelbarrows of devalued currency just to buy a loaf of bread. Hunger, homelessness, and despair became daily facts of life.

Amid this ruin, extremist voices found eager listeners. Many longed for renewed national pride and stability; demagogues offered simple scapegoats for complex problems. One such figure was Adolf Hitler, a former soldier and failed painter.

In 1920, he joined a tiny Munich group called the German Worker's Party, soon renamed the 'National Socialist German Workers' Party, also known as the "Nazi Party" for short. Gifted at oratory, Hitler seized leadership by tapping into widespread anger, weaving a doctrine of Aryan supremacy and virulent antisemitism. He blamed Jews not only for Germany's military defeat but for its economic collapse and moral decline.

Propaganda became Hitler's chief weapon. Under Joseph Goebbels, the Ministry of Propaganda saturated newspapers, films, radio, posters, and even children's books with hate. The Nazi propaganda depicted Jews as corrupt subhuman conspirators against the German nation. Propagandists cast Hitler as the nation's savior—strong, wise, and faultless. Enormous rallies, stirring speeches, and dramatic imagery created a powerful cult of personality that many Germans embraced as their only hope for resurrection.

In 1933, the Nazis leveraged the suspicious Reichstag Fire to suspend civil liberties, arrest communists and social democrats, and intimidate all opposition. Within weeks, the Enabling Act granted Hitler dictatorial powers, and democratic institutions crumbled. The regime shuttered independent newspapers and unions, outlawed rival parties, and the Gestapo used terror to enforce conformity. In 1935, the Nuremberg Laws revoked Jewish citizenship, prohibited marriage between Jews and non-Jews, and targeted other minorities—Roma, the disabled—with sterilization and secret killings. A pervasive culture of fear spread as neighbors spied on neighbors, children reported parents, and nobody felt safe.

When World War II began, Nazi Germany invaded Eastern Europe, confining Jews to ghettos before launching the "Final Solution." Death camps—Auschwitz, Treblinka, Sobibor—became factories of murder where gas chambers, shootings, and starvation exterminated six million Jews and millions of others: Roma, disabled people, political dissidents, LGBTQ individuals, and prisoners of war. This genocide was the product not of a lone madman but of a society steeped in propaganda, fear, and hate, marching in lockstep toward barbarity.

As Allied armies closed in on Berlin in 1945, survivors staggered from the camps, their emaciated bodies and broken spirits shocking the world. Hitler's Third Reich collapsed, but its ideology survived. In postwar Europe and beyond, neo-Nazi cells sprang up—in South America, the Middle East, the United States—recasting swastikas and racial theories for new audiences. Even today, Holocaust denial websites, white-supremacist groups, and extremist rallies testify that hatred endures when democracy is fragile and fear runs high.

In the 1970s and early '80s, California—a land famed for progress and diversity—became a surprising battleground for revived Nazi ideology. Rural communities suffering economic hardship and cultural change proved fertile soil. Small groups calling themselves the National Socialist White People's Party or hiding behind "heritage" slogans used leaflets, underground radio, and local paper ads to peddle racism, xenophobia, and antisemitism. Militant skinheads and survivalist communes adopted swastikas, republished Nazi texts, and held rallies guarded by sympathetic police under free-speech protections. Cross burnings, synagogue attacks, and fire bombings followed, revealing that hate need not be large to be deadly.

Northern California's logging towns, declining factories, and shifting demographics bred resentment. Neo-Nazi compounds formed in remote clearings; some posed as anti-government militias, others hoisted Germanic banners. They preyed on white working-class anxieties—blaming immigrants, minorities, and social change for economic and moral decline. Law enforcement often hesitated to intervene, leaving residents to feel besieged by armed men who pointed rifles from ridges and bullied anyone who defied them.

Yet resistance emerged too. Across the state—from San Francisco to rural foothills—coalitions of clergy, veterans, educators, students, and civil-rights activists rose to confront fascism. They organized peaceful counter-demonstrations, launched voter drives, opened cultural centers, and introduced Holocaust education in schools. Though labeled agitators or communists in some towns, they refused to be silenced, knowing that hate thrives in the absence of protest.

The clash on the Oroville ranch mirrored a larger truth: tyranny often returns in whispers, not roars, and even a handful of extremists can poison a community unless decent people stand firm. Democracy demands constant vigilance, daily acts of solidarity, education, and moral courage— especially in corners so quiet no one seems to listen. Otherwise, the shadows of the Reich will creep back, arming themselves once more in the darkness.

The lower neighbors, once embittered and withdrawn, had by now become radicalized, consumed by a toxic ideology that had bled into every corner of their existence. What began as whispered resentments and late-night radio broadcasts had metastasized into full-blown fanaticism. No longer were they believers in the lies; they embodied them. They inhaled them. Their hatred, no longer hidden in the shadows, boiled over openly, preached like scripture, brazen and unashamed.

Drawn into the orbit of the local Nazi movement like moths to a flame, they became disciples of destruction, eager students of hate. Every meeting was a sermon. Every pamphlet a commandment. With every swastika they waved, they stubbornly pushed back against a changing world they couldn't understand.

The movement gave them everything they thought they lacked: identity, purpose, someone to blame. In a world they saw slipping away, the Nazi rhetoric offered them a firm hand and a finger to point: at immigrants, at Jews, at Black Americans, at anyone who didn't fit the mold of their warped, monochrome ideal. And most recently—at the three men up on the hill.

To them, Thomas, Thomas Jr., and James weren't just

neighbors. They were symbols. Symbols of freedom, of independence, of something unbroken. Of defiance in the darkness's face that had taken root in the valley. Their presence wasn't just an affront—it was a threat. A direct challenge to the lower neighbors' belief in dominance through fear.

And so, their hatred for the family on the hill reached a fever pitch, growing louder, sharper, more unhinged with every passing day. It became ritualistic. At sunrise and sunset, one or more of them would appear on their porch, rifles in hand, standing like sentries of hate, silhouetted against the blood-red sky. They didn't need to say anything. The guns spoke for them.

They would wait for the sound of a car coming down the gravel road. As Thomas and his sons drove by, heading to town or returning from their rounds on the ranch, the lower neighbors would rise in unison, raising their rifles with theatrical precision, as if answering some perverse roll call. The weapons would track the car's motion like the needle of a compass, unwavering.

Sometimes, they'd stare through the scopes, their fingers

curled ominously near the trigger. Sometimes, they would mouth silent threats, their lips twisting with venom. Other times, they would smile—that slow, vacant, predator grin that sent ice water through the veins of anyone who saw it.

On more than one occasion, as the family passed, a rifle barrel would lift and aim directly at the windshield. In those moments, the world seemed to stop. The hum of the engine, the crunch of the gravel, even the rustle of wind in the trees—it all went still. Nothing but the sound of blood pounding in the ears and the sickening click of a trigger being pulled—not enough to fire, but enough to know: "We could."

The message was obvious: We are watching. We have weapons. And we are willing.

The family on the hill, no matter how strong their resolve, could not ignore the ever-thickening sense of danger. No longer was it simply posturing. It wasn't merely ideology or bravado. It was a slow, deliberate preparation for something worse. A storm was coming. And it was being built by the hour in the valley below.

Back on the ranch, nights grew longer and sleep harder to find. The peaceful silence of the countryside was replaced by a low thrum of dread, an emotional frequency impossible to ignore. Every sound outside became a potential threat. Every flicker of movement through the window curtains was a reason to reach for the rifle rack.

Thomas, once a man of reason and patience, now kept his revolver within arm's reach even at the dinner table. Thomas Jr., who once found solace in working the land, now walked the perimeter of the ranch twice a night, his eyes scanning the tree line. And James—young, idealistic James—had grown quiet, his fists clenched tighter with each passing day, his boyhood replaced by the hard edge of vigilance.

The lower neighbors had become something more than people—they had become agents of fear, warped by extremism into instruments of psychological warfare. They had sacrificed their humanity at the altar of hatred and now walked with the chilling confidence of those who believe themselves untouchable.

But even as the air turned poisonous, and the rifles more than props, Thomas and his sons held their ground. Because they knew what the neighbors didn't—that the only thing more dangerous than hate left unchecked… is the courage to stand against it.

And so, the ranch stood. Quiet. Armed. Waiting.

Not for revenge. Not for blood.

But when decency would have to decide whether to confront the shadows creeping over the valley—or retreat into silence once again.

Chapter 8

Day of shooting

The early morning air on November 11, 1976, was unusually still, as if the land itself were holding its breath. A thin layer of fog clung to the valley floor, wrapping the oak-covered hills in a veil of gray. Thomas and James sat in the cab of their old pickup truck; its engine humming low as it bounced along the rough, rutted driveway that snaked down from their ranch on the ridge. It was a drive they'd made hundreds of times, but today, something felt different.

The truck's tires kicked up small stones as they descended, the landscape slowly unfolding before them—the rusted fence posts, the fields dotted with frost, the low, brooding silhouette of the lower neighbor's house coming into view like a fortress hunched in the shadows. As they neared the bottom of the drive, Thomas instinctively lifted his foot off the gas, the truck slowing as his eyes fixed on the road ahead.

There, standing at the edge of his property, was the lower neighbor.

He wasn't just watching this time. He was waiting.

Clad in a heavy, oil-stained coat and boots caked with dried mud, he stood with both feet planted wide and his rifle gripped tightly in his hands, the barrel resting lightly against his forearm but angled just high enough to betray its purpose. His eyes locked onto the approaching truck with a feral intensity, the whites stark against the deep red of his face, flushed from either the cold—or rage.

Thomas felt the muscles in his neck tighten. "He's out," he muttered, more to himself than to James.

James, sitting beside him, leaned forward, peering through the fogged windshield. "Rifle again," he said, his voice low and even, though his hand trembled slightly on his knee. "Same as yesterday."

"No," Thomas said quietly. "Not the same."

There was something different in the man's stance—something deliberate, rehearsed, as though he were waiting for this moment, anticipating it. The morning light, weak and cold, glinted off the metal of the rifle as he lifted it slightly, enough for the Smiths to see that the weapon was not slung for show, but ready for use.

For over four months, the campaign of terror from the lower neighbor had escalated with chilling precision. The harassment had begun subtly—slurs muttered at passing, long stares from the porch, mysterious damage to fences and gates. But as the months dragged on and the Smiths refused to be bullied off their land, the neighbor's tactics grew bolder, more unhinged.

Gunfire had become a nightly ritual, erupting from the woods below in short, sharp bursts. Sometimes they fired into the air, other times into the trees bordering their pasture—close enough to splinter bark, close enough to send the horses running in a panic, close enough to remind them that no place was safe after dark.

Then the loudspeakers appeared, placed carefully along the fence line. They blasted scratchy recordings of Hitler's speeches, military music, and hateful propaganda. The noise climbed up the hillside and poured into the ranch house, breaking into their sleep, their meals, and even into their thoughts—like a sickness spreading through the quiet.

They had called the sheriff's department repeatedly, each time providing details, dates, even audio recordings. But the answers were always the same: *"We can't prove it came from him." "There's no evidence of direct threats." "We'll send a car around."* The deputies would drive by, speak to the neighbor politely, and then leave—while the Smiths remained behind, still surrounded by fear.

Now, as they edged past the base of the drive, the truck's tires crunching slowly over gravel, the full weight of the last four months seemed to tighten its grip around them. The neighbor raised the rifle slightly, not aiming it outright, but not lowering it either. His lips parted in what might have once been a smile, but was now something colder—cruel, calculating.

James's breath caught in his throat. "He's waiting for a reaction," he said.

Thomas didn't answer. He clenched his jaw tight, his knuckles white around the steering wheel. He kept the truck moving, steady and slow, eyes forward, refusing to give the man the satisfaction of fear. Thomas couldn't help but glance in the over where the neighbor stood, unmoving, rifle still raised—watching them with the slow patience of a predator.

It was a warning. Not a bluff. Not anymore.

The Smiths had endured months of intimidation. But this—this was different. This was a line being drawn, not in words or gestures, but in the cold steel of a rifle barrel, and the hateful glint of a man's eye who believed that no law, no consequence, could touch him.

And as the truck rumbled on toward the main road, the silence between father and son was heavier than any words they could have exchanged. They both knew what the morning had made clear:

The feud had entered a new phase.

The man below was no longer just angry. He was waiting for an excuse.

As Thomas and James approached the lower neighbor on that cold November 11th morning, the truck creaked to a stop just at the edge of the property, the dust barely settling before the sound of lower neighbor voice tore through the quiet.

"This is your last day on this earth, you Jewish nigger lover!" he screamed, his voice cracking with hate. The words echoed like a rifle shot, bouncing off the valley walls and snapping the early morning stillness like a brittle twig.

Thomas felt his heart seize. Not with fear, but with a sharp, bracing clarity. This was the moment—the confrontation they had dreaded for months had arrived, not as a slow boil, but as a sudden flash of fire and venom. The lower neighbor—face flushed, eyes wild—stood in the middle of the road with his rifle held at chest level, knuckles white, finger hovering just above the trigger.

James's breath caught, and Thomas could see his son's hands trembling at his sides, jaw clenched, eyes locked on the barrel of the gun pointed in their direction. Despite the tremor in his limbs, James didn't flinch. He stood frozen, but not broken.

Thomas's mind raced. He scanned the terrain with a soldier's instinct—the incline of the road, the angle of the lower neighbor's stance, the line of sight from the house behind him. Every variable snapped into focus.

He knew one wrong word could get them killed.

Thomas got out of the truck, stepped forward, slowly, his hands raised just above his waist—open palms, a universal sign of peace, though he doubted Ralph recognized much beyond hatred at this point.

"Neighbor, there's no need for this," Thomas said, his voice low and deliberate. "Let's talk this out like reasonable men."

The lower neighbor's eyes narrowed. His lip curled. "Reasonable? You think I give a damn about talk?" His voice was shaking now—not with fear, but with the frenzied adrenaline of someone who had convinced himself he was righteous. "I've seen the way you people look at me, up there on your high horse! With your long-haired boys prancing around like some queer hippies... You think you're better than us?"

Thomas didn't answer the insult. He kept his eyes locked on the lower neighbor. "No one's looking down on you, neighbor. We just want to be left alone. Same as you." The lower neighbor laughed—a sound more like a bark. "Left alone? I was fine before you came. Before you brought

243

your filth into this valley. You think you can just waltz into my country and poison it with your Jew friends and your mongrel kids and your faggot flag? I served too, you know. Not for this!"

Thomas could feel his chest tighten. He was a veteran. He'd seen this kind of rage before—in the eyes of men who had come back from war with nothing but bitterness left, men who found new enemies wherever they looked.

He kept his tone even. "You and I both wore a uniform. You know what that means."

The lower neighbor took a step forward, the rifle barrel twitching slightly with the movement. "Don't you dare compare yourself to me."

James, sensing the escalation, took a small step closer to his father. Thomas shot him a warning glance—Stay still. Don't move.

The sun was cresting the eastern ridge, casting long shadows through the oaks and lighting the lower neighbor's face in stark relief—every line, every twitch, every drop of spit flying from his lips, illuminated in the amber light. He looked feral. Hollowed out by hate.

Thomas tried again. "My son and I—we are not here to fight. But we will defend ourselves if we have to. You know that."

The lower neighbor laughed again, but there was something brittle in the sound. His breathing was erratic now, shoulders heaving. The gun wavered, just slightly.

"You already lost," he said. "You just don't know it yet."

And for a long moment, the world stood still.

The only sound was the wind rustling through the trees, and the distant clatter of a hawk calling overhead. A standoff older than time itself—two men and a rifle, one holding hate, the other holding the line.

The lower neighbor's grip tightened around the worn stock of the rifle, his knuckles bone white, his breath coming hard through flared nostrils. His eyes, narrow and burning with suspicion, locked onto Thomas like a predator gauging the distance before the lunge.

"Talk?" he spat. "After everything you've done?" His voice cracked with emotion, not just anger, but something more volatile—a twisted mix of paranoia and wounded pride. "You people don't deserve to be here. This is my land, my valley. And I'll do what it takes to protect it."

Thomas didn't flinch. He stood his ground, hands still raised, his body a study in calm restraint. But inside, every nerve screamed for action. He could feel James beside him, taut as a drawn wire, his breathing measured but shallow. The tension in the air was suffocating, coiled tight between the three men like a tripwire.

James, catching his father's subtle cues, stayed close but composed. He kept one eye on the lower neighbor's trigger finger and the other on the barrel, tracking every minute shift in body language. The speed at which things could go wrong was clear to him. He wasn't ready for violence—but he was prepared for it.

Thomas took a half-step forward, slow and deliberate. "Nobody's here to take your land, neighbor," he said evenly.

"We're not your enemy."

But the lower neighbor's expression twisted with scorn. "Don't lie to me, Thomas. You think I don't see what's happening? You come up here with your long-haired boys, your black friends, your *ideas*. Do you believe this is still America? You brought this sickness into my valley!"

Thomas flinched at the word *black*. He knew what Ralph was talking about—the time Thomas had stopped to talk to the old black fisherman by the Feather River. A simple moment of kindness, now perverted into a symbol of betrayal in Ralph's delusional mind.

"You don't belong here!" the lower neighbor bellowed, voice rising to a fever pitch. "You think you can replace us? Make this your playground while the rest of us rot? We built this! *My father died on this land!*"

Thomas's voice remained steady, but his eyes sharpened. "I know about loss. I fought too. I buried people too. But hate will not bring anything back. It's just going to leave you alone."

The lower neighbor laughed—a brittle, high-pitched cackle that cut through the cold air like glass. "Alone? You think

I'm alone?" His eyes gleamed now, wild and distant. "There are more of us than you think. And we're just getting started." Thomas exchanged a quick glance with James. It was more than bluster now. The lower neighbor was not merely angry; he had become radicalized.

The rifle twitched, rising a few degrees.

"I saw you talking to that nigger down by the river in town!" the neighbor roared, his voice sharp with accusation, his eyes blazing with fury. "You Jewish nigger-lovers—all of you deserve to die!"

The words cut through the morning air like a blade, harsh and violent, echoing through the trees with a venom that left the ground colder than before. Thomas's heart sank, not just from fear, but from the sickening realization that this man's bigotry had evolved into something far more dangerous than mere resentment. It had festered, taken root, and now burned hot with the kind of hatred that sought blood.

The lower neighbor's body was taut with rage, his stance no longer posturing but poised—like a man on the edge of doing the unthinkable. The rifle trembled slightly in his grip, but not from uncertainty. His hands were steady, guided by a twisted clarity that came from years of indoctrination, isolation, and hate.

Thomas stood his ground, forcing his breath to remain even though his pulse pounded in his ears. The bile in the man's voice made him want to shout back, to lash out, to strike—but he knew that one wrong move, one raised voice or twitch of the hand, could be the spark that ignited a tragedy.

He raised his hands slightly, not in surrender, but in restraint. "Neighbor, listen to me," he said, his tone low, measured, but firm. "This isn't the way. You can't let this hate control you. We live in the same valley. We breathe the same air. And we've got to find a way to live together, whether we like it or not."

The neighbor's lip curled in disgust; his face contorted into a mask of contempt. "Live together?" he spat. "With your kind? With your long-haired hippie sons and your race-mixing trash? You think you can come here, bring your filth, and pretend it's just another town like all the others you people ruined?"

He took a step forward; the gravel crunching beneath his boot; the rifle bobbing slightly with the movement. James stiffened beside his father, his eyes locked on the rifle, every muscle in his body coiled and ready. He didn't speak, didn't breathe too deeply. He knew what this was—a test of patience, a standoff of willpower. And any wrong word could turn the moment into a headline.

Thomas's mind raced. He knew he couldn't reason with hate, but maybe he could humanize himself just enough to buy time—to plant a seed of doubt, a flicker of hesitation in the neighbor's boiling mind.

"You know my name," Thomas said calmly. "You know who I am. I've never hurt you. I've taken nothing from you. I've only tried to build a life for my family. Just like you have. Is that really so different?"

The neighbor barked a bitter laugh. "Don't play innocent with me. Talking to that old nigger down by the river—what, you think I didn't see that? Must have grown up with them. You think I don't know what you're doing? Bringing them in, infecting the valley?"

Thomas swallowed hard, pushing past the pain of hearing Jeremiah's memory dragged through the dirt, of seeing human decency twisted into betrayal by a man so lost to his hatred he no longer saw people—only threats.

"You ever think," Thomas said slowly, "that maybe the only thing infecting this valley... is fear?"

The neighbor's jaw twitched, but his eyes never wavered.

James watched closely, memorizing the man's posture, the minute shifts in his shoulders, his legs—anything to predict if the rifle would rise.

The silence that followed was thick, as though even the wind had stopped to listen.

Thomas's voice lowered. "You keep this up, neighbor, and you're going to cross a line you can't come back from. Not with us. Not with the law. Not with your soul."

But there was no softness in the lower neighbor's gaze—only a simmering fury, fanned by years of resentment and stoked by the lies of men who had taught him that hate was power. His silence spoke louder than his shouting ever had. Thomas understood then: this man had chosen his war. This wasn't about land or neighbors anymore. This was about identity—about a man who believed that violence was his inheritance, and that peace was weakness.

Still, Thomas stood firm. Still, he would not turn his back.

Because in the face of such ugliness, cowardice was not an option.

And if this day ended in fire, he would meet it standing— with his son beside him, and dignity intact.

The neighbor's fury boiled, every word that had spewed from his mouth building toward something irreversible. His hands gripped the rifle with deadly familiarity, and Thomas could see it now—the minute flex in the man's trigger finger, the decision forming behind his eyes. This wasn't a bluff. This was hate sharpening into intent.

Thomas's breath caught in his chest. He could feel James's presence at his side, still as stone, waiting for any signal. They were both calculating—distance, trajectory, timing—

anything that might mean the difference between life and death. Thomas opened his mouth, ready to try once more to reach through the fog of madness...

And then, "Look out, Dad!" James's voice cut through the moment like a lightning bolt, sharp and urgent as he pointed in the direction behind the lower neighbor.

The neighbor spun around, instinctively turning his rifle toward the sound behind him. For a heartbeat, the world held still.

Behind the lower neighbor, a figure had emerged from the tree line—a man, another local neighbor from farther down the road. He wasn't armed, but the alarm in his wide eyes said everything. He had heard the shouting. He had seen the gun. Cautiously, with hands outstretched, he approached, a lone witness to the unfolding madness.

In that split-second of confusion—as the lower neighbor turned to face the newcomer, his attention fractured—Thomas acted.

"Now, James—GO!" he barked, grabbing his son's arm. They bolted.

Kicking up gravel and dust, Thomas and James sprinted for the truck, their boots pounding against the earth. Time seemed to warp as the air pulsed with adrenaline. Thomas could feel the raw instinct to survive surging through him, and James kept pace beside him, eyes wide but focused. Neither dared to look back.

The moment the doors slammed shut behind them, Thomas threw the truck into gear. The tires spun for half a second before catching the ground, and the engine roared. In the rearview mirror, the neighbor had turned back, stunned, his rifle lowered but not forgotten. He shouted something—words lost to the growl of the engine and the roar of their own blood in their ears.

Thomas didn't look back again.

When they finally crested the ridge and reached the flat ground near their ranch house, Thomas killed the engine, and the truck skidded to a stop. Silence fell, interrupted only by the ticking of the cooling engine and the ragged sound of their breath.

They sat there for a moment, hearts racing, eyes locked on

the path behind them.

"Are you okay?" Thomas asked, glancing quickly at James. James nodded, though his hands trembled. "Yeah. I... I think so."

They sat in silence, the weight of what had just happened pressing down like a thundercloud. The danger hadn't passed—not really. It had just been delayed. But in that narrow margin of time, they averted a crisis. For now.

"Who was that man?" James finally asked, his voice barely above a whisper.

"Neighbor from two lots over. Henry Keller, I think," Thomas said, still catching his breath. "God bless him for showing up when he did."

Even though Henry's house was set back from the main road, he knew the lower neighbor's behavior well over the years. Henry has seen the gradual change in the lower neighbor. He happened to be checking his mailbox on the main road when he heard the commotion between Thomas and his neighbor.

They both knew it could have ended so differently. If Henry hadn't arrived at just the right moment, if the lower neighbor's finger had flexed just a hair more, if they had hesitated instead of running—everything might have changed forever.

Thomas looked out over the hills, eyes scanning the horizon. "We need to do something. We can't just let this keep going."

James nodded silently. He could still feel the pressure of that rifle's aim on his chest. Still hear the slurs, the poison, the threat behind every word the lower neighbor had shouted.

"We will," he said.

The encounter had shattered any illusion that things might resolve on their own. The lower neighbor wasn't just angry or unstable—he was dangerous. And now there was a witness. Someone else had seen it. That meant they had a chance—maybe a small one—to get help, to be heard, to protect themselves and others.

But that would come later.

For now, Thomas put a hand on his son's shoulder. "You did good, James. You stayed calm."

James gave a faint, shaky smile. "You too."

They sat a little longer, letting the cold wind wash over them, grounding them in the hilltop's safety. And as the morning sun broke fully through the trees, warming the battered earth, they both knew one thing for certain:

This wasn't over.

But they were still standing.

"Dad... what are we going to do?" James asked finally, his voice tight, almost brittle. It was the kind of question that carried more than just concern—it held fear, and the aching hope that a father might still have all the answers.

Thomas turned to his son, studying the fear etched across his features. The boy had been brave—braver than most men— but he was still a teenager, and nothing in his life had prepared him for this kind of hatred.

Thomas placed a hand on his shoulder, grounding them both. "We'll be all right, son," he said, more firmly than he felt. "We're home now. Let's go inside and make the call."

Inside, the house felt colder than usual, as though the encounter had followed them in and set up camp in the walls. James hovered by the window, monitoring the driveway as Thomas strode to the kitchen wall phone and pulled it from the receiver. He didn't hesitate. His hands were steady, but his mind raced—reliving the lower neighbor's voice, the venom, the look in his eyes.

The line rang once, twice, and then: "Sheriff's office." "This is Thomas Smith," he said without pause. "I need to report a serious threat from our lower neighbor. He was armed and made violent threats against me and my son this morning. He aimed his rifle at us. Said we didn't deserve to live."

There was a brief pause on the line. Then the sheriff's voice, low and grave: "You say he pointed a gun at you?"

"Yes," Thomas confirmed. "He's done it before, but this time... this time was different. He said he'd kill us. If another neighbor hadn't shown up... I don't know how it would've ended."

"Was anyone injured?"

"No. But he was ready to pull the trigger. And he's been blaring Nazi propaganda. Firing rounds at night. This isn't just a neighbor dispute anymore. This man's dangerous."

There was a long sigh from the other end of the line. "I've gotten calls about him before, but nothing that sticks. No one's been willing to go on record."

"Well, I am," Thomas said firmly. "Something has to be done before someone gets hurt—or worse."

The sheriff's voice shifted slightly, from cautious to resolved. "All right. I'll drive out there myself. Talk to him face to face. In the meantime, stay safe. Don't engage him. Keep your doors locked, and if anything else happens, contact us immediately."

"Thank you," Thomas said. He hung up slowly, the finality of the click echoing in the quiet kitchen.

James turned from the window; his face lined with unease. "Is he really going to do something?"

Thomas nodded. "The sheriff said he'll talk to him. Told us to stay put. But..." He paused, rubbing his temple. "We've heard that before."

He didn't say what they both were thinking: talking would not change the lower neighbor. Not now.

They sat down at the kitchen table, the silence between them stretching long and heavy. The house felt like a refuge—but also like a bunker. The weight of uncertainty pressed in from the outside like an invisible storm.

"Should we leave?" James asked softly. "Just pack up and go?"

Thomas shook his head. "We've done nothing wrong. This is our home. And we won't let hate chase us out."

But even as he spoke the words, he felt the bitter taste of doubt creeping in. They had crossed into something deeper now—not just neighborly tension, but a genuine threat. And he knew the road ahead would demand more than courage.

It would demand resolve. Unity. And an unshakable will to protect what was theirs—not just the land, but they're right to live free from fear.

Outside, the wind stirred the trees, and the sky lightened as the clouds gave way to sunshine.

James nodded, but the fear in his eyes didn't fade. It clung to him, just beneath the surface, like a shadow that refused to lift. "I hope so, Dad. This can't keep happening. What if he tries something else? What if next time… he doesn't stop at words?"

Thomas's brow furrowed, the weight of his son's words settling heavy in his chest. He had always tried to be the shield for his family—to absorb the worst of the world before it ever reached his children. But now, there was no shielding this. The line had already been crossed.

"You're right to be worried," Thomas said softly, his voice taut with emotion. "I won't lie to you—this is serious. But we're not helpless. We'll stay alert, keep each other close, and stay in touch with the sheriff." He paused, trying to summon a strength that felt distant in that moment. "For now, let's keep our heads down and try to go about our day as normally as we can."

James nodded again, but it was clear the reassurance, however well-meant, only went so far. The fear that came from having your life threatened wasn't something you could shrug off with chores or routine. It lingered in the body—in the tightening of shoulders, in the way the eyes darted toward sudden movement, in the way silence no longer felt peaceful but charged.

Still, they both tried.

Thomas pondered the thought of ending the caregiving arrangement with Joe—not out of frustration or disloyalty, but out of fear. The escalating threats from the lower neighbor had changed everything. What began as uneasy glances and veiled remarks had turned into overt intimidation; rifles raised in plain sight.

Thomas couldn't shake the fear that something terrible might happen—not to him, but to his sons. The thought of James and Thomas Jr., still young with their whole lives ahead, caught in the crossfire of someone else's hatred, was unbearable.

As a father, his instinct was to shield them at all costs—even if that meant walking away from the land he had come to love and the responsibility he had taken on with pride. Every time he looked out over the fields, he asked himself the same question: was staying worth the risk to his family's safety?

They stepped out of the house and onto the porch, the late morning sun rising over the hills with a deceptive calm. Thomas glanced toward the empty gravel strip near the barn where Thomas Jr.'s van had been just a few hours earlier. His eldest son had left before dawn, heading into town for his shift at the processing plant—a job he'd taken on to help support the family and keep the ranch running. He hadn't been there for the confrontation with the lower neighbor, but Thomas knew the moment he got home, it would all have to be shared.

As Thomas and James walked toward the barn, the usual rhythm of ranch life resumed — only in shape, not in feeling. Even the horses seemed uneasy, flicking their ears at sounds the humans couldn't hear. James moved quietly, checking feed levels and brushing down the gelding with long, slow strokes, while Thomas busied himself reinforcing one of the paddock gates that had been sagging for weeks.

But every so often, they would both glance toward the tree line near the southern edge of their property, where the dense growth concealed the slope down to the lower neighbor's land. Every creak of the windmill, every flutter of wings in the branches overhead, sent their muscles tensing.

Thomas Jr. wouldn't return until late afternoon, dust on his boots and the faint scent of machinery clinging to his clothes. He would notice the tension immediately. The way James kept glancing out the window. Thomas stood a little straighter, more alert. The way no one smiled quite the same.

But for now, the ranch pressed on. Chores to do. Repairs to make. Lives to live.

Still, the morning's violence hung over everything—like smoke from a fire that hadn't gone out.

And as the shadows grew long again, the family moved with

quiet resolve. Aware that this land was still theirs.

But knowing now—without a doubt—that they would have to fight to keep it safe.

About an hour after returning to the house and making the call to the sheriff, Thomas stood by the kitchen counter, scanning the list of supplies he had taped to the fridge the night before—eggs, flour, coffee, canned beans, kerosene. They were running low on everything, and there was no putting it off. No matter how shaken they were by the morning's events, the ranch still needed to run, and that meant venturing into town.

James sat at the table across from him, still visibly tense. His knee bounced beneath the wooden chair, a nervous rhythm he couldn't quite stop.

"We've got to go, son," Thomas said, his voice calm but resolute. "We can't let him take this from us, too. The ranch, the town—this is still our home."

James didn't argue. He just nodded, then rose to his feet and slipped on his jacket, his eyes lingering briefly on the window, where the golden hills rolled down toward the valley. He didn't need to ask who might be watching from below.

Before leaving, Thomas ran through a quiet checklist. He stepped out to the truck and walked a slow circle around it, checking the mirrors, the tires, the back bed, making sure everything was in place and that nothing seemed tampered with. It was routine now—this simmering wariness that followed them like a shadow.

Inside, James double-checked their phones and a small first-aid kit, then tucked a flashlight and a wrench under the passenger seat—just in case. Neither of them spoke much as they prepared. The silence between them said enough.

As they climbed into the truck, Thomas paused before turning the key.

"The sheriff should be with him by now," he said, glancing briefly at James. "We'll keep to the plan—drive straight, don't stop, don't look his way. Just focus on getting there and back."

James gave a nod, his mouth a tight line. "Let's go." The engine rumbled to life beneath them, and Thomas eased the truck down the long dirt driveway. Though the high sun brightly lit the cloudless hills, the day felt anything but light. The weight of the morning clung to them, sinking into their limbs and pressing against their chests like a storm that hadn't passed.

As they neared the bottom of the drive, the familiar knot of tension returned. The lower neighbor's house began to peek through the trees, the edge of the yard just visible beyond a rusted gate and the haphazard fence line that had become his personal canvas of threats.

Thomas slowed just enough to scan the road ahead.

And then there it was.

A patrol car, parked just off the shoulder of the road, its white-and-gold doors marked with the insignia of the county sheriff. The cruiser's windows were tinted, but the outline of a deputy standing near the neighbor's front porch was visible through the gaps in the trees.

Relief — sharp and immediate — washed through them. Thomas exhaled. James let out a quiet, audible breath.

"He's here," James said.

Thomas nodded. "Let's keep moving."

As they rolled past the driveway, Thomas offered a quick, subtle nod of acknowledgment, catching the sheriff's eye for just a moment. The officer didn't wave, but he watched them pass, his face unreadable, hands resting lightly on his belt.

The lower neighbor was nowhere in sight.

They didn't linger. Thomas pressed on the gas, and the truck picked up speed as they left the scene behind. Even with the comfort of seeing law enforcement on the ground, neither man spoke for several miles. It was a relief—but a fragile one, like a window cracked just enough to let in a breeze but not strong enough to keep out a storm.

When the edge of town came into view—the gas station, the market, the hardware store—they both felt a subtle shift. Civilization. Other people. The sense that they weren't alone in this fight.

And yet, the unspoken truth hung between them: this wasn't over.

The lower neighbor had been confronted before. It hadn't changed him then. Would it be now?

Thomas pulled into the market parking lot and killed the engine. He turned to his son and met his eyes.

"Let's make this quick. And stay sharp."

James nodded. "I'm with you."

And together, they stepped out of the truck—not just to buy groceries, but to reclaim, piece by piece, the simple life they refused to surrender.

Thomas kept his rifle tucked behind the seat in the truck, the butt resting on the floorboard wrapped in a well-worn flannel. What once would have felt like an extreme precaution had, in recent months, become part of his routine—as essential as a seatbelt or a spare tire. It wasn't about fear as much as it was about readiness. Life on the ranch had changed, and no matter how much he hated it, he could no longer ignore the threat that lingered at the bottom of the hill.

He'd never imagined this life. Not here. Not on the ranch, where he'd come to rebuild, to heal. And yet, here he was— driving with a weapon, heart alert to every silhouette and shadow. James hadn't questioned it. He just accepted it, the way children quietly accept the presence of something terrifying just beyond the edge of the light.

Inside the grocery store, the fluorescent lights hummed overhead, casting everything in a sterile glow. Thomas pushed the cart while James walked beside him, each of them grabbing items with a kind of mechanical precision— flour, coffee, rice, eggs, canned beans. The list was short, but the silence between them made it feel longer.

They said little.

James hunched his shoulders, his eyes constantly flicking toward the front windows of the store, as if half-expecting to see the lower neighbor's pickup roll by. Thomas, meanwhile, moved with focus, his mind trapped in a loop of calculations—distance, escape routes, timing. He wasn't just grocery shopping. He was moving through a battlefield where any wrong step might trigger something.

The other shoppers seemed to sense it. A few offered polite nods, but no one came too close. The Smiths—once known in town for their hard work and kind manners—now carried a different energy. People could read it on their faces, in their gait, in their eyes. Something had changed.

At the register, the young cashier greeted them with forced cheerfulness. "Morning, Mr. Smith. James."

Thomas nodded, managing a thin smile. "Morning." James looked down at the floor.

The cashier didn't say another word. She rang up the groceries quickly, her eyes flicking now and then to Thomas's tired, worn face. She could tell something heavy was on his mind, even if he didn't say a thing.

When they exited the store, the bright midday sun made the world feel a little too exposed, as if even their shadows were being watched. They loaded the bags into the truck bed in silence, the metallic clang of cans and glass jars the only sound between them.

Thomas shut the tailgate with a firm thud, then turned to his son. "You good?" he asked quietly.

James didn't answer right away. Then, finally: "Yeah. Just... wish it didn't feel like this every time we go into town."

Thomas nodded. "I know. I do too."

They climbed into the cab and shut the doors. Before turning the key, Thomas reached back and adjusted the rifle, making sure it was still where he could reach it if needed. James watched, saying nothing.

The drive back to the ranch loomed in front of them—ten winding miles through quiet roads and long stretches of oak-shadowed isolation. Town had been uneventful, but the return trip meant passing the same spot they'd dreaded earlier. The memory of the lower neighbor's threats lingered like smoke in their lungs.

Thomas started the engine and glanced down the road.

"Let's take the long way home," he said, his voice calm but firm, as if distance might help settle the tension still hanging in the air.

James looked over. "Through the orchards?"

Thomas nodded. "Adds a few minutes, but it keeps us off his line of sight."

James exhaled, a small thread of tension unwinding from his chest. "Good."

And so, they rolled out of the parking lot, not in a panic, not in a rush—but with quiet resolve, knowing that for every day they managed to return home in one piece, they'd earned it.

The road ahead curved gently through the valley, a ribbon of cracked pavement flanked by golden fields. Somewhere back there, hate still sat simmering, waiting for a chance to boil over.

But in this moment, with the sun filtering through the windshield and the truck humming beneath them, Thomas and James drove on—two men tethered not just by blood, but by the growing weight of shared survival.

As Thomas and James drove the 20-minute journey back to the ranch, the landscape slowly shifted around them. The two-lane paved road, smooth and empty in the fading afternoon light, eventually gave way to a rugged dirt path that snaked through groves of oak and brush-covered hills. The transition marked the halfway point, and with it came a familiar sense of home, but also unease. They both knew this stretch too well—the sudden dips, the blind curves, the creaking sound of the suspension as the truck climbed and descended the uneven terrain.

The cab was quiet, heavy with unspoken concern. Thomas kept his eyes on the road, hands tight on the wheel, while James scanned the tree line with a quiet intensity. The silence between them wasn't strained—it was survival. Each twist in the road brought them closer to the ranch but also closer to potential danger. Ever since the incident in the morning, tensions had been escalating, and Thomas had sensed that something was coming.

About half a mile from the ranch, the road narrowed and curved sharply around a bluff where visibility dropped to nearly zero for a few seconds. It was here, at that blind turn, that it happened.

A pickup truck came barreling around the bend from the opposite direction, fishtailing in the loose dirt and swerving directly into their path. Thomas slammed the brakes, the tires screaming as the truck skidded to a stop in the middle of the road. Dust exploded into the air, cloaking both vehicles in a blinding haze.

Thomas coughed, waving the dust from his face as the particles began to settle. Then, through the thinning cloud, he saw the outline of the truck's grille and the unmistakable dents and rust patterns on the fender. He recognized it instantly—it belonged to the lower neighbor.

Thomas's pulse quickened. He glanced at James, whose face had gone pale. Before either of them could speak, the driver's side door of the opposing truck was flung open with violent force. The lower neighbor leapt out, his boot hitting the ground hard, rifle already in hand, and raised halfway.

Thomas didn't hesitate. Years of experience and instinct took over. He reached down, pulled his own rifle from the floor of the cab, and swung it up with mechanical precision. His eyes locked on the neighbor, who was now stranding outside his truck with rifle in hand with a murderous look in his eyes.

"Stay down," Thomas said to James, his voice low and firm.

The neighbor raised his rifle, but his movements were still crude, uncalibrated. Thomas had already lined up his shot. With one breath to steady himself, he squeezed the trigger.

The report of the rifle cracked like lightning through the canyon.

The bullet hit the neighbor in the side of the head with sickening accuracy. His body twitched and crumpled, the rifle falling from his hands. As he collapsed, his fingers spasmed and involuntarily pulled the trigger on his own weapon.

A single, wild shot fired across the gap, the sound echoing out like a final curse. The bullet tore through the driver's door of the neighbor's truck and struck the woman in the passenger seat—his wife. She'd been shouting something, perhaps words of encouragement or fury, but now she slumped against the dashboard, blood blooming on her blouse.

Thomas stared, chest heaving, as the weight of what had just happened began to settle on him. The entire confrontation had lasted seconds, but it felt like an eternity.

James sat frozen beside him, eyes wide, mouth slightly open. Thomas reached over and put a hand on his shoulder.

"It's over," he said, though he wasn't sure if he believed it himself.

The dust still hung in the air, but everything else was silent now—no birds, no insects, just the distant rustling of the wind moving through the trees. And the road ahead was finally, hauntingly, clear.

Thomas and James watched in frozen horror as the lower neighbor's body crumpled to the ground, landing in a cloud of dust with a dull thud. For a moment, everything seemed suspended in time. The rifle clattered beside him, and then—

barely a breath later—a second, unexpected gunshot rang out, sharp and echoing. The sound bounced off the canyon walls and vanished into the still air, leaving behind an eerie silence.

Thomas instinctively ducked, then raised his head cautiously, scanning the area for an additional threat. But there was none. His eyes landed on the neighbor's pickup. The passenger door had swung open slightly, and the woman—his wife— was slumped across the seat, motionless. A thin stream of blood trailed from her chest to the floorboard. The reflexive shot from her husband's twitching hand had struck her.

What had just happened hit Thomas all at once. The immediate relief of neutralizing the threat drained from him, replaced by a sickening wave of dismay. The confrontation had been brief, brutal, and irreversible. Two people were dead. And though he knew he had acted to protect his son and himself, the weight of it pressed on him like an avalanche.

Beside him, James sat frozen, his face pale, lips parted slightly. He turned to his father, his voice trembling. "Dad… what should we do?"

Thomas took a slow breath, steadying himself. His hands were still shaking slightly, adrenaline coursing through his system like wildfire. But his mind, honed by years of dealing with emergencies, began to clear.

"We need to call the sheriff. Right now," he said. His voice was firm, but beneath the surface, there was a current of grief and gravity.

James fumbled for his phone, fingers stiff and slow. He punched in the number and held it to his ear, glancing at the bodies, then quickly away. When the dispatcher answered, his voice cracked as he spoke, but he managed to relay the basic facts: a hostile confrontation, a threat with a firearm, shots fired, two dead.

As James gave the details, Thomas remained alert, scanning the tree line and the surrounding road, instinctively guarding against the chance that this wasn't over—that someone else might emerge from the woods, another supporter of the lower neighbor's twisted ideology. But no one came. The land had gone quiet again.

The silence between father and son returned as they waited.

Minutes passed, slow and thick. The weight of what they had just lived through hung between them like smoke. Thomas looked over at James, who sat stiffly, staring forward, jaw clenched.

Then, without a word, Thomas started the truck and gently started moving, careful to avoid disturbing anything more than necessary. The tires crunched over the dirt, and he turned the truck around, heading back toward town.

"We'll meet them halfway," Thomas said quietly. "We need to do this right."

James gave a small nod, saying nothing. He understood. This was far from over.

About ten minutes into the return drive, they saw the sheriff's SUV cresting the hill ahead. Thomas slowed, then brought the truck to a full stop on the side of the road. He rolled down his window, leaning slightly out as the sheriff's vehicle pulled up beside them.

The sheriff—grizzled and calm, with a commanding presence honed by years of dealing with backcountry conflicts—stepped out of the driver's side and approached.

Thomas wasted no time. His words came out in a rush, cracked and urgent. "Sheriff, I just shot the lower neighbor. He pulled a rifle on us. I had to do it. He was going to kill me and my boy."

The sheriff's face shifted immediately into a sober expression. He nodded once, eyes narrowing as he absorbed the gravity of the situation. "All right, Thomas," he said carefully. "I hear you. I'll follow you back to the scene. Let's get this handled the right way." Other sheriff cars speed past with emergency lights flashing.

Without further questions, he motioned for Thomas to lead the way. They drove in solemn silence, the sheriff's SUV trailing a few car lengths behind.

When they arrived at the scene, flashing lights were already visible through the dust and brush. Deputies had beaten them there—dispatched the moment James finished his call. Yellow tape was going up, officers marking evidence and keeping bystanders at a distance.

Thomas parked and climbed out slowly, arms raised slightly in a show of cooperation. The sheriff met him at the front of the truck, his expression unreadable.

"I'll need to hear it all," the sheriff said. "From the beginning."

Thomas nodded, and with James standing silently nearby, he recounted everything—the sudden ambush, the rifle, the threat to his son, the fateful shot. He spoke clearly, but without embellishment. There was no need for dramatics. The truth, brutal as it was, stood on its own.

When he finished, the sheriff gave a slow, deliberate nod. "You did what you had to do," he said. "But we still have to follow protocol."

Thomas expected it. When the cuffs clicked around his wrists, he didn't flinch. The cold metal felt like confirmation—not of guilt, but of gravity. This was real. This was happening. The patrol car door opened with a mechanical click, and Thomas ducked inside, sparing one last look at James.

James stood still, watching his father disappear behind the tinted window. The deputies didn't speak to him right away—they were busy cataloging the scene—but the unspoken message was clear: he was on his own now, at least for a little while.

As the vehicle pulled away, James remained standing on the side of the dirt road, dust rising in swirls around his boots. He knew what he had to do. There were calls to make. Family to reach out to. He had to hold it together, for his dad, for the ranch, for everything that might come next.

Thomas Jr. pulled up to the scene after hearing about the shooting at local Radio Shack in Oroville, which had a police scanner on. He was shocked to see the shooting and his dad handcuffed in the back of a patrol car. James got into Thomas Jr's van, still in shock at what he just witnessed.

Meanwhile, in the back seat of the patrol car, Thomas stared out the window at the hills he'd known for the past year. The sun was starting to dip low behind the ridge. He had no idea what the days ahead would bring. But deep down, beneath the fear and the sorrow, there was a quiet, resolute belief: he had done what was necessary to protect his son. And for that, he would answer to the law—but not with shame.

Chapter 9

Trial

The sheriff's car rumbled down the long, winding road toward the county jail, its engine a steady growl in the otherwise, quiet afternoon. The tires crunched over the gravel with a rhythm that might have been calming on any other day. But for Thomas, every bump in the road felt like a jolt to the chest.

The landscape passed by like a memory—soft rolling hills coated in golden grass, patches of oak and pine trees casting their long shadows as the sun slid lower in the sky. The wind stirred the branches gently, and the leaves shimmered in the fading light, oblivious to the storm churning inside the man in the back seat. To anyone else, it would have looked like a peaceful drive through the countryside. For Thomas, it felt like a slow procession into the unknown.

Bound at the wrists, he sat rigidly in the back seat; each turn of the car sent a fresh wave of pain through his wrists. He stared out the window, trying to anchor himself in the familiar—the fence lines he'd mended, the trails he'd walked with James, the old windmill that hadn't turned in years. He tried to let the scenery calm him, to remind him of who he was before this day, before the blood and the gunfire and the weight of a decision no one ever wants to make.

But the peace of the landscape couldn't quiet his thoughts. The haunted-memories, fears, what-ifs. He thought about the moment the lower neighbor stepped out of that truck, the way the sun had caught the metal of the rifle just before Thomas raised his own. He thought about James's voice, tight with fear, and the look in his son's eyes as the dust settled around them. Most of all, he thought about the two bodies lying still on that dirt road, the brutal finality of it all.

He knew that he had done what was necessary. Any hesitation would have meant death—his or his son's. But the clarity of that moment was already being fogged by the uncertainty of what came next. Would the sheriff believe him? Would the DA? Would a jury? And even if the law ruled in his favor, how would his community respond? Politics, ideology, and personal relationships divided them, and news spread through their small town. Some would call him a hero. Others would call him a murderer.

He shifted in his seat, the motion stiff and uncomfortable. A smell of dust, leather, and engine oil permeated the car's interior. Since leaving the scene: The sheriff hadn't spoken, and the radio was off. The quiet was a gift, a precious respite that allowed him to sort through the chaos in his head.

Up ahead, the red and blue flashes of police cruisers cut through the fading daylight like the beat of a warning heart. With sirens wailing and engines gunning, they returned to the scene, urgency evident in every movement. More deputies. More tape. Additional questions. The wheels of justice were already turning, grinding forward with cold efficiency. Each siren was a stark, blaring reminder of the weight of what had happened.

Thomas clenched his jaw. His hands were still cuffed in his lap, his fingers stiff and sore beneath the metal. He forced himself to breathe. Panic wouldn't help him. Regret wouldn't change anything. The only thing left to do was face what lay ahead—whatever that might be.

A hawk drifted overhead, its wings spread wide, catching a thermal rising off the hills. Thomas watched it for as long as he could, wishing he could soar above it all—above the land, the fear, the weight of consequence. But there was no escaping now. The road led only to a cold, fluorescent-lit room where questioners would interrogate, writers would document, and judges would make their pronouncements.

As the sheriff made the last turn toward the county jail, the familiar wooden sign appeared at the edge of the lot. *County Sheriff's Department & Jail—Serving Since 1889.* The words had always felt distant before, like part of a system that didn't concern him unless he was renewing a permit or signing off on a livestock report. Now they loomed large.

The patrol car pulled into the gravel lot and came to a stop with a heavy sigh of brakes. Thomas took one last look out the window at the setting sun streaking across the western sky. The land was beautiful, eternal, indifferent.

The door opened.

"All right, Thomas," the sheriff said, his voice gruff but not unkind. "Let's get this part done."

Thomas stepped out of the car, his boots hitting the gravel with a crunch. He stood tall, even as the cuffs remained on his wrists. Whatever was coming next, he would face it head-on.

He thought back to his childhood in Mississippi, to the thick summer air filled with the hum of cicadas and the scent of freshly turned earth. He remembered his father's calloused hands and the quiet wisdom in his mother's voice. That small, unassuming town where he was raised had given him more than just a start—it had given him the foundation for who he became. It was there, beneath the weight of the southern sun and the expectations of hard days, that he had learned the values that shaped him: hard work, honesty, self-reliance, and a deep respect for others, even those he didn't agree with.

Those values had been tested more than once over the years. They carried him through lean times, family struggles, and the slow, often unforgiving work of building something that would last his family, too — he had built that with care, with long nights and quiet compromises and a love that had outlasted hardship.

But today, all of it—everything he had worked for, everything he had built—was hanging in the balance. The simple peace he had fought to preserve now felt like a fragile illusion. The gunfire, the blood, the silence after—those moments had shifted something inside him, as if the ground itself had cracked beneath his boots.

Thomas's thoughts spiraled back to the lower neighbor. The image haunted him—The lower neighbor's body folding awkwardly to the dirt, limbs slack, a puff of dust rising like smoke from the dry road. The shot had echoed for only a second, but the memory of it lingered, loud and heavy in Thomas's mind. He hadn't wanted to pull that trigger. God knew he hadn't. But in that split-second, with a rifle aimed at him and James beside him, there had been no choice.

It started with mutterings—politics, grievances, conspiracy talk. Then came the swastika flags on his property, the aggressive movements, the not-so-subtle remarks when Thomas, James, or Thomas Jr would drive by. And finally, threats—veiled at first, then spoken aloud. The lower neighbor had begun shooting toward the ranch and playing Nazi marching music and Hitler's speeches over a loudspeaker. Thomas had filed reports, made calls, tried to keep things civil. But the lower neighbor's anger kept growing, fueled by something dark and twisted.

And the lower neighbor's wife—Thomas didn't know what to make of her. She had once been quiet, a background figure at local functions. But lately, she'd stood alongside her husband, just as loud, just as hard-eyed. She had chosen that path, too. Still, her death weighed on him. Whether or not she had pulled a trigger or not, she hadn't deserved to die in that way—in a random, reflexive flash of violence.

Two people gone. Two lives ended on a quiet stretch of dirt road in the hills. And no matter how justified it had been, no matter how clear the danger had seemed in the moment, Thomas couldn't shake the guilt. It clung to him like wet clothing, heavy and inescapable. He didn't feel like a man who had defended his son. He felt like someone who had stepped over a line and wasn't sure he could find his way back.

His life, everything he had built, had shifted in an instant. There would be investigations, news coverage, judgment— some of it fair, some not. His name would be spoken in whispers at church, over coffee, across gas station counters.

And no matter the outcome, no matter what the law decided, the truth of the matter was this: nothing would ever be the same again.

The sheriff allowed Thomas his one phone call, as required
by law. Thomas nervously picks up the phone and dialed the
ranch owner Joe Cook's phone number. Joe picked up on the
second ring, his voice calm and steady, but with an edge of
concern already in it. "Thomas, is that you?"

"Yeah, Joe, it's me," Thomas said, his voice tight, cracked
around the edges. There was a long pause as he collected
himself, the dull hum of the fluorescent lights above his head
filling the silence. His fingers trembled, still slick with the
faint residue of ink from the fingerprinting. It felt like he was
calling from another world.

"I'm in the county jail," he added, ashamed to even speak
the words aloud.

Joe didn't speak right away, but his silence was heavy with
understanding. "What happened, Thomas?"

Thomas exhaled, trying to steady himself, trying to keep the
guilt and the grief from overwhelming his words. "The lower
neighbor," he began. "He cut us off on the road—me and

James. Jumped out of his truck with a rifle. He was ready to shoot. I... I didn't have a choice, Joe. I grabbed mine. Got him before he could raise it. It was quick."

He stopped, his throat tightening as he thought of the aftermath.

"The lower neighbor's wife was in the truck," he added, quieter now, as though saying it softer might change the truth. "When he fell... his rifle went off. She was hit. Died right there in the passenger seat."

Joe let out a breath, long and pained. "Christ."

"I didn't see her," Thomas said, his voice cracking. "I didn't even know she was there until after. It was like everything happened in the space of a single breath. Then it was just... silence."

The line went quiet for a long moment.

"You, okay?" Joe asked.

Thomas looked around the room—bare walls, scuffed

linoleum, the scent of antiseptic and stale air. A young deputy stood near the desk, watching him, arms crossed over his chest.

"No," Thomas replied honestly. "But I'm holding on."

Joe didn't offer false comfort. That wasn't his way. "This is bad, Thomas, but I know you. And I know you wouldn't pull that trigger unless you had to."

Thomas closed his eyes for a moment, grateful for the words but still burdened by the reality. "James witnessed the whole thing." "I keep seeing his face. He was scared, Joe. I don't know what this is going to do to him."

"You protected your son," Joe said. "You did what a father is supposed to do."

Thomas nodded to himself, trying to absorb those words, to let them anchor him.

"I need a lawyer," Thomas added, his voice returning to the present. "Someone who can handle something like this. Someone who won't flinch."

Joe said, "I'm going to make some calls." "I know a guy in Chico—excellent reputation, tough as nails. I'll get him headed your way. And I'll check in on James. Make sure he's not alone."

"Thank you," Thomas murmured. "I don't know what I'd do without you right now."

"You'll get through this," Joe said. "One step at a time."

The line went quiet again. There were no more words, not really. Just the weight of what had happened and the uncertain road ahead.

Thomas hung up, the receiver clicking into place. The deputy approached and nodded once. "We'll take you to a holding cell now."

As the handcuffs clicked back onto his wrists, Thomas didn't resist. He stood up, his shoulders squared not from pride, but from resolve. He wasn't sure how this would all play out— how the law would judge his actions, how the community would react—but one thing was certain: the fight for his freedom, for his family, and for the truth was just beginning.

And he would meet it head-on.

Following the call, they guided Thomas down another sterile corridor with a scuffed and dull linoleum floor from years of weary footsteps. The fluorescent lights overhead flickered, casting a pale-yellow hue on the walls that seemed to close in with every step. The deputy said little—just motioned with a nod as they approached the last door on the left.

The metal door creaked open with a mechanical groan. It was a simple room, no bigger than a feed shed—concrete floor, cinderblock walls, a steel bench bolted to the wall, and a narrow-barred window set high above eye level. The kind of place built to strip a man down to the essentials. No privacy. No comfort. Just time, and the thoughts that came with it.

As Thomas stepped inside, the deputy closed the door behind him. The sharp clang of the lock sliding into place echoed down the hallway and into Thomas's chest like a drumbeat. He didn't flinch, but the sound carved another notch in the growing sense of isolation. He was alone now. At least, in the physical sense.

He sat down on the cold bench, the metal unforgiving beneath him. He leaned forward, elbows on knees, fingers laced together, and stared at the small rectangle of light from the barred window. It offered only a sliver of the outside world—just a patch of sky, streaked with the last colors of dusk, giving way to night.

Time passed in the cell. There were no clocks, no noise except the inaudible murmur of boots outside or the low murmur of a voice down the corridor. The hours dragged on, each one longer than the last. Thomas lost track of whether it was night or just late evening. The sterile lighting overhead never dimmed, never changed. It created a sense of timelessness that gnawed at him.

He replayed the events of the day again and again—every detail, every breath. The moment the lower neighbor's truck appeared, the flash of the rifle barrel, the sound of the gunshot, and the sudden, awful silence that followed. He thought about the lower neighbor's wife, about James, about the way everything had changed in the blink of an eye. The decisions he'd made. The finality of them.

And then, the silence would creep back in, heavy and thick

like fog settling over a field.

At times, he buried his face in his hands, pressing his palms into his eyes as though he could force the memories out. Other times, he stared at the floor, jaw clenched, trying to find logic in it all—some way to file the chaos into neat compartments that would make it easier to carry. But it never worked. The weight of it was constant. Oppressive. Like trying to breathe with a boot on your chest.

But through it all—cutting through the gloom like a distant, flickering light—were Joe's words: *"You're not alone."*

They echoed in his thoughts, simple and steady, a quiet refrain. Thomas held onto them like a rope in a flood. He repeated them to himself, over and over, trying to let them take root against the flood of doubt and guilt. Joe would find a lawyer. He'd check on James. Some people outside still believed in him—still understood he wasn't a violent man, but one forced into an impossible situation.

He took a slow breath and leaned his head back against the wall, the cold concrete grounding him. There was no comfort in the cell. No softness, no mercy. But there was still a sliver of hope. As small as that window above him. As faint as the dying light, it let through.

He closed his eyes, not to sleep, but to rest. Just for a moment. Because tomorrow, the real fight would begin.

As the investigation at the scene of the shooting unfolded, a clear emerging picture of what had transpired began to emerge. The quiet, rural stretch of dirt road—usually empty save for the occasional passing pickup or grazing deer—had become a hub of lights, law enforcement, and slow, deliberate movement. Yellow crime scene tape fluttered in the night breeze, cordoning off the area where two lives had ended just hours earlier.

Floodlights set up by county deputies lit the area with a harsh, unnatural glow. The peaceful sounds of the countryside were gone, replaced by the quiet buzz of radios, the clicks of camera shutters, and the steady voices of investigators taking notes. Forensic experts moved carefully, shining flashlights on every surface as they examined footprints, shell casings, and blood patterns—documenting every detail with precision.

Investigators found the lower neighbor's body just outside the driver's side door of his truck, with a rifle near his outstretched hand. Blood pooled beneath him in a dark, sticky patch, now congealing under the night air. The forensic team had confirmed what initial observation suggested: the bullet had entered through the side of his head, a clean shot delivered from a distance. The shattered driver's side window of the truck, the angle of the trajectory, and the location of lower neighbor's body all aligned with Thomas Smith's account.

Inside the truck, investigators discovered the lower neighbor's wife; her lifeless body was slumped against the door. The bullet wound that ended her life had come from her husband's own rifle. The evidence was tragically clear— her death had not been intentional, but it was no less final. A single, accidental shot, triggered by the spasms of a dying man's hand, had taken her life before she could even cry out.

From the sequence of physical evidence, a coherent narrative began to take shape. The lower neighbor had driven aggressively, cutting off Thomas and James Smith on the narrow road. He had exited the vehicle with a rifle, matching the accounts of past harassment and confrontations. In that moment of escalation, the lower neighbor had reached into the cab to grab his weapon, and Thomas, fearing for his life and the safety of his son, had reacted with a single, decisive shot. The rifle in the lower neighbor's hands had discharged in a final, involuntary reflex—unleashing the bullet that claimed his wife.

Investigators reviewed the long, troubled history between the two families—filled with complaints, sheriff's reports, and statements from neighbors. The lower neighbor had a reputation for provoking and making threats. Still, seeing two bodies lying in the dirt—a husband and wife—was heartbreaking. It was a scene that went beyond reports and evidence, speaking to a deeper tragedy that logic alone couldn't explain.

Detective Carla Rivas, one of the lead investigators on the scene, stood near the back of the Smiths' truck, her notepad resting at her side. She watched as the evidence techs placed the weapons into sealed bags, their latex gloves glinting under the floodlights. She had seen her share of shootings over the years, but this one weighed heavier than most.

"This wasn't just another argument," she murmured to the

deputy beside her. "This was a pressure cooker that finally blew."

The deputy nodded. "Town's been on edge for a while. Folks taking sides. Lines getting drawn deeper."

Rivas looked back at the taped-off perimeter. "Well, now it's spilled over. And two families are going to feel this for the rest of their lives."

Despite the mounting evidence pointing to self-defense, no one could ignore the complexity of what had happened. Two people were dead. A man in custody. A son traumatized. And a community already strained by ideological divides now faced with a tragedy that could fracture it further.

The legal case would not be easy. Some in town would defend Thomas, calling him a father who did what he had to do. Others would focus on the loss of the lower neighbor— especially his wife, who never pulled a trigger, never left the truck, and yet died just the same. There would be public statements, vigils, protests, maybe even threats. The court would navigate the facts, but the community would struggle to reconcile the human cost, a far more difficult task.

As the night wore on and the forensic team completed their work, the floodlights began to shut down, one by one, leaving the land once again in darkness. But the scars left behind—both physical and emotional—were just beginning to show.

Back at the county jail, Thomas sat hunched in his cell, his shoulders heavy with the weight of everything he couldn't control. The hours dragged by in an endless blur, the sterile air pressing in on him like a weight. The cold, hard bench beneath him had long since numbed his body, but the ache in his chest only deepened.

He rubbed his temples, trying to slow his racing thoughts, but they churned without pause. Images looped in his mind like a broken film reel — the lower neighbor's snarling face, the flash of the rifle, the recoil of his own shot, the horrible silence afterward. And then, James. The memory of his son's face—staring back at him through the dust and shock, his eyes wide and uncomprehending—haunted Thomas more than anything else.

James hadn't asked for any of this. He was just a kid trying to help his father with chores, trying to grow up right. And now he'd seen a man die. He'd seen his father shoot him. That kind of memory didn't go away, never. Thomas wished he could hold his boy, tell him it was over, that he was safe now. But he couldn't. Not from here. He didn't even know if James had gotten back to the ranch, if Joe had reached him, or if he'd had to wait alone in the dark for news that might never come. He knew Thomas Jr. would get off of work and take care of James.

He leaned back against the wall, staring at the small barred window overhead. Pale morning light was beginning to seep in, turning the concrete walls from cold gray to dull beige. Another day had come, and with it, the inevitable reckoning.

Later that morning, the cell door opened with a clank. A deputy gestured for him to stand. "Let's go, Mr. Smith. The sheriff wants a word."

Thomas followed in silence, his boots echoing on the linoleum floor. The corridors smelled of coffee and disinfectant, and the flickering ceiling lights gave everything a sickly glow. They stopped at a closed door, which the deputy pushed open before motioning him inside.

The room was plain and sparse—just a table, two chairs, and a small window with the blinds drawn halfway. Sheriff Dunley stood near the wall, arms crossed, while a detective sat at the table, a notepad open in front of her. Neither sheriff looked hostile, but there was a grimness to their expressions, the kind that came from handling more tragedy than anyone should have to.

Thomas sat slowly as the deputy closed the door behind him. The chair creaked under his weight.

"Morning, Thomas," the sheriff said, his voice low. "This is Detective Rivas. she's with the county's violent crimes division."

The detective, a woman in her mid-forties with tired eyes and a focused demeanor, gave a slight nod. "Mr. Smith. We'd like you to walk us through what happened yesterday—step by step. Just take your time."

Thomas took a breath and began.

He spoke calmly, carefully, recounting the escalating tension with the lower neighbor over the past several months. He told them about the threatening remarks, the gunfire above the ranch at night, the almost nightly loud speaker blasting Nazi marching music. Thomas also explained the threat on his life the morning of the shooting. He explained how he had tried to file complaints, tried to avoid conflict, tried to keep the peace. But peace had walked away the moment the lower neighbor had pulled that truck in front of him and James.

Then he described the scene in vivid detail—the cloud of dust, the way the lower neighbor had exited his truck, the glint of the rifle in the fading light, and the fear that had seized him when he realized his son was in the line of fire. His voice broke slightly as he described firing his own rifle, and the horror that followed—the sudden, reflexive shot that had claimed the lower neighbor's wife.

Detective Rivas stayed quiet the whole time. She nodded once in a while, scribbling notes on her pad, her face calm and hard to read. When Thomas stopped talking, the room went still. The silence lingered, heavy and unbroken for a long moment.

Finally, she spoke.

"Mr. Smith," she said evenly, "we're still reviewing all the evidence, but based on the forensic work at the scene and your statement—which matches what we've found—it appears this was a case of self-defense. The lower neighbor was armed and acted aggressively. And based on witness accounts and prior complaints, there's a documented history of him threatening you."

Thomas nodded, though her words brought little relief.

"However," she continued, "because there were two fatalities, and because this incident involves the use of lethal force, the case will still proceed through the courts. The DA will want a full report. There will be hearings, then a trial. And I need you to understand, Mr. Smith—it's going to take time."

The sheriff, still silent until now, stepped forward. "It's not about guilt or innocence, Thomas," he said. "It's about due process. There are folks out there who'll be looking to twist this into something it's not. You just tell the truth. Let the evidence speak."

Thomas met their eyes, resolute but weary. "I will. I've got nothing to hide."

Rivas gave him a small nod. "Your attorney will be allowed to review the full case file once it's compiled. In the meantime, we will transfer you to the county holding facility until your bail hearing.

Thomas stood slowly as the deputy returned to escort him out. The process was just beginning—he knew that now. He wasn't walking out of here today or tomorrow. But he would walk out, eventually. He had to believe that.

And until then, he'd hold on to the only thing he had left: the truth, and the hope that it would be enough.

Days turned into weeks as the investigation dragged on at a slow, steady pace. The early chaos of the incident faded, replaced by stacks of paperwork, long interviews, expert reports, and routine procedures. Each step moved the case forward, but the emotional weight grew heavier for everyone involved. The town, once a peaceful place where neighbors waved from porches and chatted over coffee, now felt like a community holding its breath—quiet, tense, and shaken.

Lines were drawn, often unspoken but unmistakably present. At the diner to front lawns, and in church parking lots, whispered conversations grew louder. Some people—many of whom had known Thomas for the past year—stood firmly in his corner. They pointed to the lower neighbor's long history of anger and intimidation, to the reports filed, the sheriff's warnings, the confrontations that had grown increasingly dangerous. To them, Thomas was a father who did what any man would have done when his child's life was on the line.

But others—especially those who had known the lower neighbor and his wife viewed the outcome through a different lens. They mourned the sudden, brutal loss of two people they'd shared holidays and town fairs with. The wife, especially, became a symbol for those struggling to understand how things had spiraled into violence. Her death, unintentional as it may have been, had struck a chord. There were those who saw her as collateral damage in a feud that had spun out of control. They asked difficult, painful questions: Couldn't there have been another way? Had it really come to this?

As public opinion shifted and swirled, Thomas's lawyer—

John Moore, an experienced attorney from Chico—worked hard behind the scenes. He carefully reviewed every police report, gathered witness statements from neighbors who had seen the lower neighbor's past threats, and collected records of the complaints Thomas had filed over the past year. He even hired a ballistics expert, who confirmed that the path of the bullets matched Thomas's story exactly.

"The facts are on your side," John said during one of their meetings. "You acted to protect your son. That's not just defensible—it's human."

Thomas nodded but said little. He appreciated the legal clarity, the strategy, the professionalism. But facts didn't lessen the guilt. Every night in his bunk, he stared at the ceiling of his cell, replaying the moment repeatedly. The raised rifle. Firing the shot. The silence. He knew he had acted fast, maybe even perfectly under pressure—but the result was still the same. Two people were dead. One child forever changed.

Joe Cook remained a steady presence, visiting the jail twice a week with updates from the ranch and the outside world. He brought Thomas slight comforts—books, letters from the kids, sometimes a photo of the horses or the barn. More than that, he brought words Thomas needed to hear.

"You did what you had to, Thomas," Joe said during one visit, gripping the bars. "You did what any father would've done—you protected your boy. If it were me, I'd have done to the end the same. I'm with you, all the way."

That support was important. So did the letters from his daughter, the occasional calls from family, and the visits from James—though those were the hardest. James tried to be brave, but Thomas could see the trauma etched into his son's youthful face. It broke his heart, knowing he couldn't undo what his boy had witnessed. He could only hope the boy saw him not as a killer, but as a protector who had no other choice.

As the court date approached, the case spilled beyond the borders of their small town. Word had gotten out—first through local papers, then to state outlets, and finally onto national news. Headlines splashed across websites and TV screens: *"Father Shoots Neighbor in Rural Showdown," "Double Death in Self-Defense Case Raises Legal Questions,"* and *"Tragedy in the Hills: A Community*

Divided."

Reporters descended like a flock of crows, their vans parked along Main Street, their cameras angled at the courthouse and the sheriff's office. Microphones were thrust at townspeople who didn't want to speak. Rumors and theories flew like wildfire—some accurate, many not.

The trial quickly became a flashpoint for bigger conversations—about self-defense laws, property rights, and the growing political and social tensions in rural America. National newspapers ran opinion pieces. TV commentators argued over whether the use of force was justified.

Protesters showed up with signs—some standing behind Thomas, others calling for "Justice for the lower neighbor's wife."

Thomas, meanwhile, kept his head down. His lawyer had advised him to stay silent, avoid the cameras, and let the facts speak in court. And that's exactly what he did. He refused interviews, declined statements, and focused instead on what he could control: his composure, his honesty, and his belief that he had done what was necessary to save his son.

But no amount of preparation could fully ease the weight in his chest. Because beneath the public spotlight, beneath the legal strategies and public commentary, there remained a very real and private truth: no matter what the verdict would be, no matter how the court ruled, nothing could undo what had happened on that dirt road.

And now, with the trial looming like a storm on the horizon, Thomas knew the hardest days were yet to come.

The day of the trial arrived with a gray, overcast sky that seemed to mirror the weight in Thomas's chest. A damp chill hung in the air as he left the transport van; officers led him up the courthouse steps. The building loomed ahead, its stone facade solemn and unyielding, like a monument to judgment. Reporters clustered at the entrance, camera flashes lighting up as he passed, escorted by deputies. He kept his head down, jaw tight, jaw locked against the noise and scrutiny.

Thomas hesitated for a moment, looked up at the reporters and said, "the truth shall set me free".

Inside, the courtroom buzzed with murmurs, tension

vibrating in the air like a taut wire. Neighbors, friends, and strangers—many knowing both Thomas and the lower neighbor for years—filled every seat in the gallery. Some had come out of loyalty. Others out of curiosity. Some came to mourn. Others came to pass judgment.

Thomas took his seat at the defense table, his heart pounding a slow, steady rhythm against his ribs. His lawyer, John Moore, sat beside him, calm and composed, flipping through his notes one last time. Across the aisle, the prosecution team settled in—confident, crisp, and focused. The judge entered, and the room rose to its feet.

Then it began.

The opening statements were like two stories unfolding in parallel—each rooted in the same day, the same dirt road, but told through vastly different lenses.

John Moore spoke first. Adjusting his jacket, he stood and addressed the jury with steady confidence. He began with the history: the months of harassment, the documented threats, the uneasy tension that had been building between the Smiths and the lower neighbor. He outlined the sequence of events with careful precision, walking the jury through each step—from the lower neighbor's sudden appearance on the road, to the raised rifle, to the shot fired in defense of a son's life.

"This is not a case about vengeance," Moore told the jury. "This is a case about survival. Thomas Smith did not choose violence—he was forced into it by a man who had terrorized his family and escalated a confrontation to the point of no return."

Moore revealed that both lower neighbors were card-carrying Nazis affiliated with a local Neo-Nazi organization.

But when the prosecution rose, the tone shifted.

They didn't dispute that the lower neighbor had been aggressive. They didn't deny the gun in his hand. But they pointed again and again to the wife's death. Her face—framed in old family photos—was shown to the jury, smiling, warm, maternal. They called her the unintended casualty of a conflict that, they argued, didn't have to end in blood.

"The lower neighbor was a bully," the prosecutor said. "But

the wife was not. And now she is dead. Because one man decided to pull the trigger before anyone had a chance to walk away."

The words stung. Even though Thomas knew what had happened, knew he hadn't meant for the wife to die, hearing the prosecution reduce the moment to a question of restraint tore at him. The look on the jurors' faces was hard to read—some stoic, some visibly emotional.

The trial stretched on for weeks.

Witnesses took the stand—neighbors who had seen the lower neighbor pacing the property line with a shotgun, store owners who remembered the lower neighbor's drunken rants. One testified to hearing him say, "One of these days, I'll take care of that bastard Smith for good."

James was called, too. He stood tall despite the shaking in his hands, and his voice wavered as he recalled the day—the dust, the fear, the way his father had acted fast to protect him. His testimony was heartfelt and raw, and it stirred a visible shift in the room.

Forensic experts backed up the ballistics report: the path of the fatal shot matched exactly what Thomas had described. As for the second bullet—the one that hit the lower neighbor's wife—it had been fired from a downward angle, consistent with the lower neighbor's position as he fell. It appeared the shot had gone off by accident, likely as he hit the ground.

The prosecution also called character witnesses—old friends of the lower neighbor—who spoke warmly about his wife, describing her as kind, loyal, and often misunderstood. One witness even claimed that the lower neighbor's violent behavior might have been caused by untreated PTSD. It added a layer of complexity to the story, but it didn't take away from the real threat he had posed.

Throughout it all, Thomas sat silently, stoic but haunted. He listened to every word. Every accusation. Every memory of the people who had died that day. His fingers clenched beneath the table, but he never raised his voice. He didn't need to. The truth, he hoped, would speak loud enough on its own.

The tension in the courtroom was so great it felt like it could snap in half when closing arguments were delivered. John Moore's last words to the jury were simple: "This was a tragedy. But not a crime. Thomas Smith didn't want to take a life. He wanted to save one."

Then the waiting began.

The jury deliberated for hours that turned into days. The courthouse fell into a tense rhythm—lawyers waiting, family members pacing, reporters clustering outside for updates that never came. Inside his holding cell, Thomas tried not to hope too hard. He'd seen enough life to know that the truth didn't always win.

But he also knew he had nothing left to give. He had told his story, stood by it, and carried the weight as best he could.

And now—whatever came next—was in the hands of twelve strangers, sitting in silence behind a closed door, deciding whether Thomas would return home... or remain behind bars for the rest of his life.

Finally, the day of the verdict arrived. Heavy clouds filtered the morning light as people again gathered inside the courthouse, the same building that had, for weeks, become a crucible for grief, anger, and uncertainty. The pew-like benches were packed to capacity—friends, reporters, neighbors, and silent observers who had come to witness the end of a trial that had gripped the entire region and captured the attention of the nation.

Thomas sat at the defense table in his worn suit, his hands tightly folded in his lap, the cuffs of his shirt a little frayed. His lawyer, John Moore, sat next to him, calm but focused, one hand resting on a stack of legal papers that now seemed unimportant. Across the room, the prosecutors wore the same carefully neutral expressions, but the slight tension in their shoulders revealed they were waiting anxiously for what would come next.

The judge entered, and the room rose. Everyone took their seats as the bailiff called the jury.

Twelve jurors filed in slowly, each step echoing through the silent room. Their faces were blank—stoic masks carved by days of intense deliberation. Thomas scanned their expressions, searching for any flicker of reassurance, but there was none to be found. His heart pounded in his chest;

his breath was shallow. He had told the truth. He had lived the truth. But the truth didn't always win. He had seen that before.

The foreperson stood.

"In the case of the State of California versus Thomas Smith," he said, holding the verdict slip in his hand, "we, the jury, find the defendant... not guilty."

The words fell like a stone into water—silent at first, then rippling out.

For a second, no one moved. It was as if the room needed time to absorb what had been said. Then, Thomas exhaled a breath he hadn't realized he'd been holding. A wave of relief, immense and unshakable, washed over him. His hands trembled in his lap as Moore placed a firm, reassuring hand on his shoulder.

The judge nodded solemnly. "Mr. Smith, you are free to go."

Whispers and soft sobs filled the courtroom as his family— James, his daughter Susan, Thomas Jr, Ron, Betty, Mel, and

Joe Cook—rose from their seats in the gallery and came forward. James was the first to reach him, wrapping his arms tightly around his father in a hug that said more than words ever could. Susan followed, eyes red, her hands gripping his like she never wanted to let go.

"You're coming home," she whispered.

Joe stood nearby; his face serious but proud. "I told you the truth would hold," he said quietly. "And it did."

Thomas nodded, overwhelmed. The room spun slightly— not from fear, but from the sheer emotional exhaustion of it all. He had survived the trial, survived the public scrutiny, the long nights, the whispered judgment. He had stood in front of the law and walked away with his name intact.

But even in that moment of exoneration, he knew that not everything had been made whole. The tragedy hadn't vanished. The lower neighbors were still gone. Gunfire and bloodshed still stained the land. And the town—fractured by grief, loyalty, and opposing narratives—would need time, maybe years, to find its way back to itself.

The courtroom began to clear as people filed out, murmuring quietly. Outside, reporters clustered near the courthouse steps, cameras ready, eager for a comment. But Thomas didn't speak. He didn't wave, didn't smile. He simply walked down the steps with his family beside him, breathing in the fresh air like a man coming up from underwater.

There were no parades, no applause. Just the steady sound of his boots on the pavement and the cool wind moving through the trees.

And though the nightmare of the trial was finally over, Thomas understood something else with deep, aching clarity: the journey wasn't truly done. The emotional scars would remain stitched invisibly beneath his skin. He would live with the weight of that day for the rest of his life—when everything changed, when life demanded an impossible choice, and he made it.

But now, at least, peace came from knowing the truth had been revealed.

And for the first time in a long time, he could walk forward without looking over his shoulder.

Chapter 10

Mississippi Whisper

Though the trial concluded, Thomas grappled with the uncertain future. The courtroom had closed its doors; the jury had spoken, and the cameras had begun to pack up and drift away—but the silence that followed wasn't peace. It was the strange, uncertain quiet that settles in after a storm, when everything is still standing, but nothing feels quite the same.

The future stretched out before him like a blank canvas—daunting in its emptiness. For months, survival had consumed every waking moment, court dates, strategy sessions, moments of doubt, and long, sleepless nights. Every ounce of his energy had gone into defending himself, preserving his freedom, and protecting his family's name. And now that the verdict had been read, and the world wasn't waiting on him to explain or justify or endure—he found himself at a loss.

He had cleared his name. But he hadn't yet reclaimed his life.

For the first time in a long time, there were no court orders telling him where to be. No deputies guarding his every movement. No reporter with a notepad waiting for a quote. He stood free, and yet the very idea of freedom now felt abstract—like something he'd imagined for so long that it no longer felt real.

He thought of the ranch. The fields that had grown wild in his absence. Months had passed since anyone touched the tools. The animals likely missing his steady presence. It had once been his place of peace, his sanctuary. But now, it felt like a question mark. Could it still be that place again? Could he walk the fence lines without seeing the lower neighbor's truck, or sit on the porch without replaying the shot?

And what about James? The ordeal has changed his son. Hardened in some ways. More grown than his years should've required. They had leaned on each other in the darkness—but now, in the light, they would have to find a new rhythm. A new way to live. Together, but different.

Thomas knew the town wouldn't all welcome him back with open arms. There would be people who looked at him differently now. Some would avert their gaze, unsure of how to speak to a man who had taken a life. Others would stare too long, hungry for answers to questions he no longer wanted to answer.

There was work to be done—emotional work, spiritual work. Forgiveness to seek, maybe not from others, but from himself. He would need to find a way to make peace with what had happened on that dirt road—not erase it, but carry it without letting it define him. That would take time. Maybe more than he expected.

But not all was uncertain.

He still had his family. James, Thomas Jr, Susan, and Ron. The people who had stood by him when things were at their darkest. Their love had never wavered. And that, he realized, was his foundation. Not the ranch. Not the courtroom verdict. Them.

Maybe he'd start small. Mending fences—veritably, and figuratively. Sitting down with James and just *being*. No courtroom pressure. No headlines. Just time. Maybe, someday, he'd walk into town again—not with his head bowed, but with quiet pride. And maybe—just maybe—he'd plant something new in the soil behind the house. Something that would take time to grow.

Because now he had time.

The question of what came next was still unanswered, but for the first time in a long while, it didn't terrify him. It called to him. Not like a warning, but like an invitation.

And Thomas, free, was ready to accept it.

As the days passed and the dust of the courtroom settled, Thomas found himself drifting more and more into memory. Without the constant noise of the legal battle to drown them out, the quieter parts of his mind stirred to life—pulling him backward, toward the red clay roads and soft drawls of his childhood in Mississippi.

Thomas would let go of the ranch caretaking job and return it back to its owner, Joe Cook. Joe understood and supported Thomas's decision.

Despite everything that had happened in his life—the joy of building a family, the ache of loss, the trauma that had nearly broken him—Mississippi had remained a place of deep, unshakable significance. It wasn't just where he had been born. It was where he had *become*.

He remembered the old house, whitewashed and a little crooked, with a sagging porch and steps that creaked under the weight of summer nights. The smell of magnolia trees still lingered in his memory—sweet, heavy, and eternal. That smell was more than fragrance. It was a presence. It was *home*.

The image of the river came next—slow-moving and wide, carving its way through green fields and whispering through reeds like an old friend telling stories. He could almost hear the plop of skipping stones, feel the cool water sliding over bare feet, the way the air always seemed just a little thicker, like it held the weight of the past in it.

Those were the days when life was simpler, though never easy. When hard work was a given, but so was community. People once settled problems with a handshake or a long walk down a dirt road. When his parents' voices filled the house with laughter and lessons, and when the biggest burden he carried was whether the rain would come in time for the crops.

Those memories had always stayed with him, like ghosts—sometimes comforting, sometimes haunting. He'd carried them westward when he left, packed between the ribs like bones of his character. Over the years, he'd visited Mississippi in dreams more often than in real life. He always meant to go back, but the ranch, the family, the responsibilities—they kept him rooted in California.

But now, something felt different.

Now, in the trial's wake and the long, bruising months of public scrutiny and private anguish, that old, familiar longing for Mississippi had grown stronger. Not just as a place, but as a refuge. A compass. A reminder of who he was *before* the world got so complicated.

Not that he wanted to escape. He wasn't running from guilt—he had faced it. He wasn't hiding from the town—he had stood his ground. But he felt called—called by the land that had raised him, by the voices of those long gone, by the slow rhythms of a life that had once centered him.

It was as though Mississippi wasn't just a memory anymore. It was calling him home—not forever, maybe, but for a while. To rest. To heal. To remember who he'd been before, the world asked him to pick up a gun.

He didn't tell anyone at first. Not even James. He just found himself sitting on the porch of a house he rented at dusk, staring out at the horizon, thinking about the way the fireflies used to light up the grass down south. He'd close his eyes and hear the old hymns from the country church he'd gone to as a boy, and feel the itch of river mud drying on his legs.

It wasn't just nostalgia—it was something much deeper, something rooted in the soul.

A whisper from the soil of his past.

And for the first time in a long while, he thought maybe he needed to answer it.

His family was settled now—grown, grounded, living lives of their own. Ron had built a successful restaurant business and was raising two kids of his own. Thomas Jr., always the wanderer, had found his rhythm managing an electrical power plant project up north. Susan was training to be an engineer in college with the same quiet wisdom she had inherited from her father. And James—James had grown into a man. Steady. Thoughtful. He carried the weight of what they had been through, but he bore it with grace and quiet strength. James's business thrived and continues to flourish.

He was glad Betty had found someone who truly saw and appreciated the kind, vibrant woman she was. She and Mel had gotten married six months earlier, and from everything Thomas could tell, they were genuinely content—settled into a quiet happiness that suited them both.

Thomas watched them all with a heart full of pride. A wave of relief and gratitude washed over him as he contemplated his children's fine qualities. They didn't need him the way they once had. That realization, once so frightening, had now become a comfort. He had done his job. He had loved them, protected them, guided them through the hardest storms. And now they were standing tall on their own.

For the first time in years, Thomas felt the space to breathe. Actual space. He could finally step back from the long grind of responsibility—the unrelenting worry, the endless need to hold everything together. That pressure, once so central to his identity, had eased. He turned inward to tend to the parts of himself that he had neglected for too long.

With his family's full support, Thomas decided after months of consideration. He would return to Mississippi—not just as a visit, but as a pilgrimage. A return to his roots. A chance to reconnect with the land, the people, the memories that had shaped him before life demanded so much of him. He wasn't running away; he was returning home—to a place that still held his name like a whisper in the trees.

The day of his departure arrived with the soft hush of morning light filtering through the trees. His house was calm, filled with the aroma of coffee and the quiet murmur of conversation as his children gathered to see him off. There were no speeches, no big moments—just the quiet reverence of a family recognizing the end of a chapter.

They stood together in the driveway; the truck packed with bags, a small cooler of sandwiches, and a worn leather-bound journal Susan had slipped into his things when he wasn't looking.

One by one, he embraced them.

Ron was first—strong and solid, his grip firm. "You've earned this, Dad," he said, voice steady.

Thomas Jr. gave him a long hug and a crooked smile. "Send us a postcard. And maybe don't fish the whole damn river dry while you're down there."

Susan kissed him on the cheek, her eyes shining with emotion. "Promise you'll write. And rest. Really rest."

And James—James stood last, quiet but composed. He stepped forward and hugged his father, holding on longer than the others.

"You sure you're okay?" he asked.

"I am," Thomas whispered. "I need this, son. But it's not forever."

"I know," James replied. "I get it."

Thomas pulled back and looked him in the eyes. "You take

care of your yourselves. You've got more in you than you know."

James nodded. "So do you."

There was laughter, too—light, healing. A shared knowing that they were strong enough now to say goodbye, even if just for a while.

Thomas stepped into his truck, rolled down the window, and looked out at the faces he loved most. "I'm not saying goodbye for good," he said. "I'll come back to visit. But I need this time for myself. To reconnect with where I came from."

They nodded, each of them feeling the truth of it deep down. And then, with the engine humming beneath him and the sun beginning to rise, Thomas turned onto the road. As the house grew smaller in his rearview mirror, he felt a strange mix of sorrow and serenity. The road ahead was long and unknown, but it was his to travel now.

And for the first time in years, he wasn't carrying the weight of a trial, or fear, or obligation.

He was carrying something simpler—hope.

The three-day drive back to Mississippi was long, stretching across quiet highways, forgotten towns, and wide-open skies. But for Thomas, the solitude wasn't a burden—it was a soothing balm. For the first time in months, maybe even years, there was no one asking questions, no courtroom tension, no deadlines or decisions looming over him. It was just him, the open road, and the hum of the truck beneath his hands.

He drove without rushing, stopping when he felt like it—at gas stations with dusty screen doors, roadside diners serving fried catfish and coffee, and long overlooks where the horizon seemed to go on forever. Lost in thought, he rode in contemplative silence. As the miles passed, Thomas felt as though he were peeling off layers of something heavy and worn. The tension in his shoulders began to fade. The worry that had dug so deep into his bones loosened its grip. His thoughts became quieter, more centered.

He passed fields of golden wheat, cotton that danced in the wind, and weathered barns leaning slightly against time. There was something comforting in the familiarity of it all.

This wasn't the California he had known—sharp hills and dry wind and fast-moving lives. This was different. Slower. Steeped in memory.

And then, just after noon on the third day, the sign appeared: *Welcome to Mississippi.*

Thomas slowed down without thinking, his eyes lingering on the weathered state line marker. It wasn't fancy—just a standard green sign with white block letters—but it hit him harder than he expected. A soft ache stirred in his chest, like the return of something long buried.

As he crossed the line, it felt like crossing into a different version of himself. Not just a place, but a part of his identity that had gone dormant beneath the responsibilities of adulthood, parenthood, and everything the world had demanded of him. Mississippi wasn't just where he'd grown up—it was where he had learned *how* to grow.

The air felt fresh—thicker, richer smelling of pine and wet earth. The sky stretched wider, the light softer, hazier. He rolled down the window, letting the breeze rush in. It carried with it a thousand memories: the splash of the river, the crackle of fireflies in tall grass, the rustling of trees that whispered secrets on summer nights.

He took a deep breath, and for a moment, he was a boy again—barefoot and laughing, a fishing rod over one shoulder, a tin of bait in his hand. Seeing his mother calling him in for supper, he noticed his father smoking on the porch, nodding at him with quiet approval. He saw friends he hadn't thought of in decades, and places that had long since changed or disappeared. But the feeling—the *feel* of home— was still there. Unchanged.

The roads grew narrower now, lined with willow trees and cottonwoods. He passed by churches with hand-painted signs, a faded gas station that looked the same as it had when he was a teenager, and a stretch of land where he once helped a neighbor bale hay under a thundercloud.

He turned onto the gravel road leading to the old family plot—land the Smiths had owned for generations, though much of it had long since been sold off or reclaimed by the woods. A few structures still stood, bones of buildings that had once held laughter, meals, and hard-earned sleep.

He parked near what remained of the old house, stepping out onto the soft, red soil. The wind rustled through the tall grass, and a bird sang somewhere in the trees. Thomas stood there for a long while, hands in his pockets, just listening.

This place didn't need to explain itself. It didn't care about trials or headlines or what people thought of him. It was— and always had been.

A place of beginning.

And maybe, just maybe, a place for a new beginning too.

Settling back into Mississippi felt less like starting over and more like *returning* to something fundamental—something buried but never forgotten. For Thomas, it was as if a piece of his soul had been waiting all these years in the red clay, in the rustle of the cottonwoods, in the slow bend of the river. The town, with its cracked sidewalks and fading paint, was quieter now, aged by time and memory. But the bones of it were the same. And that familiarity gave him something he hadn't felt in a long while—ease.

He rented a small, weathered house just a few miles from

where he had grown up, tucked behind a curtain of trees that offered shade and solitude. The porch sagged a little. The floor creaked when he walked. But he smelled the right air, and crickets, distant thunder, and the soft, timeless quiet of the deep South filled the nights.

The slower pace of life suited him. There were no court appearances, no deadlines, no town meetings full of tension. No one stopped him on the street to ask for a comment or cast a sideways glance. Here, he was just *Thomas* again— not a defendant, not a symbol. Just a man trying to remember how to live.

Each morning, before the heat settled into the bones of the land, he'd wake early, brew a cup of coffee on the stove, and make his way down a gravel path that wound through the trees to the riverbank. The water moved, glittering in the morning sun, catching light in all the right places. He'd take a seat on an old tree stump, bait his hook, and cast a line into the current.

And then—he'd wait.

Sometimes he'd catch something, sometimes not. But the

fish weren't the point. The river had always been his thinking place, even when he was just a boy with a bent rod and too-big boots. Sitting there, surrounded by the smell of pine and water, he let his mind wander. He didn't fight the memories anymore. He let them come.

It was here, at this very river, that he and Jeremiah had shared countless days as boys. Jeremiah had been his best friend—more like a brother. They'd fished from sunup to sundown, skipped rocks across the surface until their arms ached, carved their names into trees, and dreamed up grand futures.

"We're gonna leave one day," Jeremiah used to say, grinning beneath a straw hat that hardly fit his head. "Gonna see the entire world and fix it too."

They had believed it, believed in the power of hope, of possibility. Teachers, soldiers, and community leaders were all careers they considered. They didn't know then how cruel the world could be.

That dream had died with Jeremiah.

He had been seventeen. Thomas still remembered the day it happened. Jeremiah had gotten into a dispute with a local man—a petty argument that should've ended with words, maybe a shove. But Jeremiah was black in a time and place where that still cost you everything. The violence that ended his life came fast and brutal, without justice. Without apology.

Thomas had never forgotten.

Even now, as a grown man with decades between him and that day, he felt the sting of it like a fresh wound. Jeremiah's absence still echoed in his life—in the things he had done, and more so in the things he had *not* done. He carried that memory with him always, and here, by the river, he let himself feel it fully. He said Jeremiah's name out loud some mornings, soft and steady, as if speaking it might bring him closer.

"Wish you could see this, Jeremiah," he murmured once, as the current pulled at his line. "Wish you were sitting right here with me."

The river said nothing in reply, but the breeze that lifted

through the trees felt almost like a hand on his shoulder.

Thomas didn't believe in signs, not really. But he believed in presence. And he knew Jeremiah's spirit had never left this place.

As the days turned into weeks, the stillness of the river and the quiet of the land began to heal something inside Thomas. He didn't have answers for everything. He still carried scars. But he was beginning, piece by piece, to reclaim something he thought he had lost forever—his peace. His sense of belonging. His ability to breathe without flinching.

And in that small house, by that wide river, under the watchful gaze of the past, he remembered not just who he was, but who he had always hoped to be.

The memories of Jeremiah's lynching haunted Thomas, even after all these years. The pain had dulled with time, like an old wound scabbed over and weathered by decades, but it had never genuinely healed. It lived beneath the surface— quiet, persistent, always present. Sometimes it surfaced in dreams, sometimes in the silence between thoughts. And sometimes, like now, it came with the sound of the river.

He remembered the day as if it had happened yesterday—the way the town seemed to hold its breath afterward, the way the grown-ups averted their eyes, how some pretended it hadn't happened at all. But Thomas had seen the truth. He had seen Jeremiah's body hanging from a tree close to where they used to fish. He had seen what hatred could do, how it could erase a life so full of promise without consequence, without remorse. And he had felt the rage—burning hot and directionless, a boy's fury in a world that had no intention of giving him answers.

That day had cracked something inside him. Not just his heart, but his understanding of the world. Childhood ended for Thomas not with a slow transition, but in a single, brutal instant. Jeremiah had been his best friend—more than that, he had been a reflection of who Thomas might have become in a better world. Brave. Bright. Unafraid to speak the truth, even when it cost him.

The helplessness Thomas felt in the aftermath had followed him into manhood. It shaped how he viewed fairness, justice, and silence. When others whispered, it made him speak up. It made him suspicious of those in power, cautious of institutions that claimed righteousness but failed to act. And it taught him, torturously, that loss is not always loud—sometimes it's quiet, and that quiet can echo for a lifetime. He had carried Jeremiah's memory like a weight for so long that he had stopped noticing its heft. It was just a part of him—something woven into the fabric of who he was.

But now, sitting beside the river where they used to cast lines and tell stories, Thomas felt something shift.

He didn't cry—he had cried long ago, when no one was looking—but grieved honestly. He spoke Jeremiah's name out loud, not with the anger that had once laced his voice, but with reverence. As if calling him back into the moment, not to mourn him, but to honor him.

"I'm sorry," Thomas whispered. "I should've done more. I didn't know how. I was just a kid, and they—" He paused, swallowing hard. "They killed you, Jeremiah. And the world just moved on like it didn't matter."

The river kept flowing, indifferent but constant.

For the first time in his life, Thomas allowed himself to forgive—not the act, not the people who had committed it—

but himself. He had been just a boy. Powerless. Grieving. Afraid. There was nothing more he could have done. And carrying the guilt for all these years hadn't brought Jeremiah back. It had only kept Thomas chained to a past he couldn't change.

But now, by the water they once shared, he felt something like grace begin to settle in.

He wasn't letting go of Jeremiah's memory—never. But he was learning to hold it differently. Not like a wound, but like a light. Not like a scar that burned, but like a story worth telling.

Jeremiah deserved to be remembered—not just for how he died, but for how he *lived*. For the way he laughed, wide and free. They shared dreams of world travel and building a life they could be proud of. He showed courage, even when it wasn't necessary. That's the part Thomas wanted to carry forward.

He sat for a long while; the sun dipping lower in the sky, shadows stretching across the ground. And for the first time, the memory of Jeremiah didn't make him clench his fists. It made him breathe deep. It made him feel rooted. Whole.

Maybe this was what healing looked like—not forgetting, but remembering in a way that gave back instead of taking away.

Chapter 11

Connection of Life

As Thomas continued to reconnect with his past, it wasn't just the land and the memories that wrapped around him—it was the people, too. Faces he hadn't seen in decades reappeared, some changed beyond recognition, others familiar. Each interaction was like unearthing an old photograph, the kind with frayed edges and fading ink, but still full of meaning.

Then, one afternoon at the local market, something happened that he hadn't expected. He was standing in the produce aisle, eyeing a bin of late-summer peaches, when he heard a voice behind him—warm, lilting, indisputably familiar.

"Well, I never thought I'd see *you* back in town."

Thomas turned, and there she was.

Christine.

His high school sweetheart.

Seeing her again was like a jolt of electricity and warmth all at once. Silver streaks now highlighted her hair, which she pulled back in a loose bun. Her face bore the graceful lines of a life fully lived. But her eyes—those same bright, knowing eyes—hadn't changed a bit.

"Christine," Thomas said, a slow smile spreading across his face. "I can't believe it."

She laughed, tilting her head. "Well, believe it. I heard you were back. Figured I'd run into you eventually, though maybe not between the squash and the sweet potatoes."

He chuckled. "Seems about right."

What started as small talk became something deeper. They lingered by the market stalls, blocking the aisle without noticing. It wasn't just polite curiosity; it was something real, something that stirred like embers reigniting after a long rest. They swapped stories—about kids and grandkids, heartbreaks and homecomings. Christine told him about her late husband, a kind man she'd married not long after Thomas left town, and how she'd lost him five years back after a long illness. She'd raised three children, had six

347

grandchildren, and was now spending her days tending a small flower garden and volunteering at the local library.

Thomas shared the contours of his life—the ranch, the family, the trial. He didn't go into all the details, but Christine didn't need them. She listened without judgment, her eyes soft with understanding, her hand brushing his arm when his voice trembled.

By the time they left the store, the sun was hanging low in the sky and their carts were half-forgotten. He walked her to her car, and before she climbed in, she hesitated.

"I don't hardly ever say things like this," she said, "but… I'd like to see you again. If you'd like that too."

Thomas didn't even have to think. "I would."

They met for coffee the next morning, and then again, a few days later for a walk by the river. What began as cautious companionship blossomed into something steady and natural. There was no pretense between them. No need to impress or explain. They had lived enough life to understand the value of presence, of simple joys, of showing up as you are.

With Christine, Thomas felt something he hadn't felt in a long, long time—ease.

She didn't try to fix him or offer hollow reassurances about the past. She just listened. Sometimes she made him laugh so hard his sides hurt. Other times, they sat in silence, letting the cicadas sing while the sky turned from blue to gold.

They fell into a rhythm—easy, unhurried. Two people with weathered hearts finding comfort in familiar company. Their conversations spanned everything from old classmates to favorite recipes to books they had never finished. And sometimes, when the moment was just right, Christine would reach over and place her hand over his, grounding him in the here and now.

Thomas hadn't expected this. He hadn't come back to Mississippi looking for love or even companionship. But here it was, quiet and unexpected, offering itself like a second chance. A chance not to erase what had come before, but to begin again—with someone who understood the value of each moment.

And in that, Thomas found something he never thought he'd feel again: hope—not just for peace, but for joy.

A few months later, on a crisp autumn afternoon, the Mississippi sky stretched wide and brilliant above Thomas and Christine as they walked side by side along the familiar riverbank. The trees lining the water had turned to gold, amber, and russet, and with every step, leaves crunched beneath their boots in soft, rhythmic bursts. The breeze carried the earthy scent of fallen leaves, wood smoke, and damp soil—autumn in its purest form.

Thomas breathed it in like medicine.

They walked in comfortable silence for a while, Christine's arm frequently brushing against his, her scarf fluttering in the wind. The river moved slow and steady beside them, the sun dancing across its surface in fractured glints. It was the same river where Thomas had once fished with Jeremiah, where he had come to grieve, to heal—and now, it had serenely become the backdrop to something new. Something whole.

He had found peace here, yes. But more than that, he had found Christine. And with her, the promise of a future he'd never expected.

Thomas glanced at her as they walked. The cool air flushed her cheeks; she tucked her hair beneath a wool cap; and her eyes—the same eyes he'd fallen in love with so many years ago—held a calm, content light. She looked happy. And he knew, then and there, that he didn't want to imagine the rest of his days without her beside him.

Without overthinking it—without rehearsing or waiting for the perfect moment—he stopped. The leaves rustled gently around them.

Christine turned to look at him, confused at first. "Everything all right?"

Thomas smiled. "More than all right."

And then, intentionally, he knelt down on one knee.

Christine's hand flew to her mouth as she gasped softly, her eyes widening with realization.

"Christine," he began, his voice low and steady, but full of emotion, "I've loved you since we were kids. That never went away. Life took us down different roads, but it brought us back here, to this place, and to each other. No more waiting for me. I don't need time to be sure. I have made up my mind. Will you marry me?"

For a moment, the only sound was the wind moving through the trees and the river whispering beside them.

Christine's eyes filled with tears as she nodded, her voice a soft whisper. "Yes, Thomas. I will."

He stood, and she threw her arms around him, holding him firmly as if they could somehow catch up on all the years they had missed. They kissed, there beneath the canopy of trees, with the golden light of the afternoon spilling through the leaves like confetti. It wasn't grand, and it wasn't staged—but it was perfect.

They married a few weeks later in a quiet ceremony at the courthouse. Neither of them wanted anything flashy or complicated—just something real. Something true. A few close friends attended, including some childhood classmates, neighbors from town, and Joe Cook, who made the trip from California to stand at Thomas's side as his best man.

An old friend, Reverend Hank Morris—who used to pass them notes during homeroom and later found his calling in the ministry—officiated the ceremony. His voice trembled with emotion as he pronounced them husband and wife.

Christine wore a simple cream dress with a lace shawl draped around her shoulders. Thomas wore a clean white shirt and a charcoal jacket. They didn't exchange expensive rings, just plain gold bands, symbols of a love that didn't need decoration.

Afterward, they held a small celebration at their new home— a cozy red-brick cottage nestled at the edge of town, surrounded by tall mulberry and fig trees whose branches swayed in the late-autumn breeze. The scent of slow-cooked greens and cornbread filled the kitchen, and laughter echoed off the porch as old friends shared stories and toasted the newlyweds with sweet tea and peach wine.

It wasn't a lavish affair. But it was full of warmth. Of joy. Of second chances.

Later that night, after everyone had gone, Thomas and Christine sat on the porch beneath a quilt, watching the stars come out one by one. The night was quiet but alive—the kind of silence that doesn't feel empty, but full. Full of everything that had come before, and everything still to come.

Thomas looked over at his wife and smiled.

"I never thought I'd be here again," he said.

Christine leaned her head on his shoulder. "Me neither. But I'm glad we are."

And in that moment, beneath the Mississippi stars, with the smell of wood smoke in the air and her hand in his, Thomas felt something deep and enduring settle in his chest.

Not just peace.

Not just hope.

But home.

A sense of tranquility enveloped him, a quietude that was both beautiful and profound. Thomas and Christine embraced each day with quiet gratitude, finding joy not in grand adventures or plans, but in the small, shared moments that stitched their lives together. Their mornings began with coffee on the porch, watching the sun climb through the trees, and ended with slow dances in the living room to the sound of old records spinning under soft lamplight.

They spent their days gardening side by side, their hands in the dirt, nurturing rows of vegetables and flowering vines. Thomas built raised beds from reclaimed wood while Christine charted the seasons in a weathered journal, her neat handwriting recording what thrived and what didn't. The blackberry bushes behind the house grew wild and full each summer, their dark fruit sweet and sun-warm. Christine would tie a scarf around her hair, grab two baskets, and the two of them would head out, arms brushing, laughter rising through the branches as they plucked the ripe berries.

Sometimes they'd talk for hours—about childhood memories, their children, their dreams for the years ahead. Other times they moved together in comfortable silence, two souls long acquainted, content just to *be* in the same space.

The red-brick house became more than a home. It became a sanctuary. A place where the wounds of the past slowly healed beneath soft light and shared love. The chaos of the world—the noise, the judgment, the politics, the tragedy—stayed outside. Inside was warmth. Safety. A love that had taken root meticulously, but thoroughly, blossoming with the patience of two people who knew what it meant to lose and had learned to cherish what they had.

But life, as always, had its own plans.

Ten years into their marriage, Christine began to slow. At first, they thought it was just fatigue. Maybe the flu. Maybe age catching up. But when the tests returned, a doctor, long experienced in delivering bad news, discreetly and objectively announced cancer. It came rapidly and without mercy.

The diagnosis was late. The treatments were tried, but the cancer had already spread, burrowing into bones and lungs and liver. It took Christine's strength before either of them was ready. One day, she was trimming rose bushes by the porch; the next, she was too weak to stand on her own.

Thomas never left her side.

He sat through every appointment, every scan. Throughout her chemotherapy, he held her hand, rubbed her back when she was nauseous, and read to her on days she was too weak to keep her eyes open. Late at night, when pain and insomnia plagued her, he whispered stories into her ear. He told her about the first time he'd seen her—how he'd tripped over his own feet at the County Fair just trying to catch a better look. She'd laughed even then.

When home care was no longer enough, hospice took over. A nurse set up a bed in the front room where the sunlight streamed through in the afternoon. Christine wanted to face the garden, she said. She wanted to watch the light move through the blackberry bushes, even if she couldn't walk to them anymore.

Her last days held only quiet. With goodbye. With soft-spoken love. And when the time came—when her breath slowed to a whisper and her hand stilled in his—Thomas sat beside her, forehead resting against hers, tears falling silently.

357

He stayed with her long after the nurse had left. The house, once so alive with their laughter and music, now felt cavernous in its silence.

Losing Christine was a blow he hadn't expected. Even after all he'd endured in life—the trial, the losses, the grief of his youth—this was different. This was *now*. This was *her*. She had been his companion in healing, his second chance, the hand that held his without judgment. And now she was gone.

In the days that followed, Thomas moved through the house like a ghost. The creak of the floorboards echoed too loudly. The kitchen smelled too clean. Her scarf was still hung on the back of the chair by the door. And the blackberry bushes—overgrown and unruly—swayed in the wind like they were waiting for her to return.

He tended them anyway. Every morning, he walked out and picked the ripest berries, placing them in the basket she had once used. He didn't eat them. He just needed to keep the ritual alive.

The house, though emptier now, still held her. In every corner. Within every room. Within every musical note and worn page of her favorite book. And Thomas, though brokenhearted, held on to that. To her presence. To the love that had changed him.

He wasn't ready to move on.

But he was learning how to carry her with him.

As Thomas approached his eightieth birthday, life in Mississippi—once his refuge, his sanctuary—was becoming harder to manage. The river still flowed gently in the mornings, and the blackberry bushes still bloomed in season, but his body no longer moved with the ease it once had. Tasks that had once brought him peace—walking the length of the gravel driveway, harvesting vegetables, even rising from his favorite porch chair—had become daily trials.

The aches in his joints were deeper now, more persistent. His hands, once steady and sure, had trembled moderately. The steps leading up to the red-brick house seemed taller each day. And the silence, once comforting, had felt heavier with each passing night.

His children—especially Susan—saw the changes. They

visited whenever they could, taking turns flying in, cooking meals, and handling small repairs. But each visit ended the same way: with quiet looks passed behind his back and hushed conversations in the kitchen, full of concern they didn't want him to hear.

It was during one of those visits, on a quiet Sunday afternoon in early spring, that Susan finally brought it up. They sat on the porch, just the two of them, wrapped in shawls against the fading chill. The sky was soft with clouds, and the garden below was just beginning to wake up after winter's sleep.

"Dad," she began, her voice gentle but steady, "you know we love having you here. This place… it means a lot to all of us. But we're worried."

Thomas didn't respond right away. He watched a pair of birds picking at the feeder, their feathers fluttering in the breeze. He already knew what she was going to say. Part of him had known for a while.

Susan reached over and placed her hand on his. Caring for yourself is becoming more challenging. You don't always say it, but we see it. The missed calls. The empty fridge.

When James arrived, he found you alone, attempting gutter repairs.

He smiled. "Didn't fall off the ladder, did I?"

"No," she said with a soft chuckle. "But you could have."

He nodded, his fingers curling around hers. "So, what are you suggesting?"

Susan leaned in, her expression both loving and firm. "I've got that apartment built into the basement of my house—the one with the separate entrance. It's private and the perfect place for you. You'd still have your independence, but I'd be close by if you needed anything. You wouldn't have to be alone anymore."

Thomas looked out at the yard, at the rusted garden tools leaning by the shed, at the empty rocking chair beside him. He thought of Christine's laughter echoing off these walls. He thought of Jeremiah, of the river, of all the years he'd spent trying to find peace and how, somehow, he had.

And yet... he knew she was right.

"I swore I'd die in this house," he said after a long pause. "I came here to put down roots. To rest. To feel close to the parts of myself I'd left behind."

Susan nodded, not interrupting.

"But I never expected to live this long," he added, smiling with tired eyes. "And I sure didn't plan for the day when I couldn't make it to the damn mailbox without getting winded."

They both laughed, the moment lightened by humor but not robbed of its weight.

He turned to her, his voice quiet. "It's hard, honey. It's hard to let go of something that's been home. That's felt like the one place I still belonged."

"I know," she said. "And we'll come back here, Dad. As much as you want. We'll take trips and spend weekends. This place will always be yours. But it's time we take care of *you* the way you've always taken care of us."

Thomas swallowed hard, the emotion catching startlingly in

his throat. He looked at her—his daughter, steady and kind—and felt the swell of love and gratitude rise within him.

But the truth was undeniable. The stairs were harder to climb. The aches lingered longer. Some mornings, he would sit on the edge of the bed and wonder how long it would take just to tie his shoes. He hadn't wanted to admit it, but the signs were clear. The land had nurtured him, yes, but now it was also asking more of him than he could give.

"All right," he said. "All right, Susan. Let's make it happen." She squeezed his hand, her eyes glistening with relief. "Thank you, Dad."

They sat for a while longer, watching the sky shift colors as the day wound down. No more words were needed. They had decided—not with regret, but with grace.

Later that evening, as Thomas packed the first of his belongings—Christine's favorite books, the carved wooden frame that held a photo of all his children—he felt something unexpected: peace. A chapter was ending, yes, but a new one was beginning. One where he'd be close to family, surrounded by love, and held up by the people he had helped shape.

Mississippi had been his return.

But now, it was time to go home again.

At first, Thomas resisted the idea with quiet stubbornness. Mississippi had been more than just a place to live—it had been his refuge, his reckoning, and his redemption. He had buried pieces of himself in that red earth, healed wounds by the riverbank, and loved again in the small brick house that had once felt like the last stop on a long, hard journey. The thought of leaving it behind stirred something deep in his chest—a sadness that settled in his bones.

Susan's voice echoed in his mind during those quiet moments: *"You wouldn't be giving up your independence, Dad. You'd be choosing a different kind of freedom—one where you're not alone."*

He knew she was right.

And the thought of being near his children again—of having

dinner with Susan and her husband on a Sunday evening, of hearing the laughter of his grandchildren in the backyard—offered a comfort he hadn't realized he was craving.

A few weeks later, the decision was made.

His sons, Thomas Jr. and James, arrived to help with the move. They arrived with boxes, rented a U-Haul truck, and brought strong backs and kind eyes. Together, they sorted through the rooms of the red-brick house—folding Christine's quilt, wrapping picture frames in old newspapers, and boxing up well-worn paperbacks and chipped mugs with memories clinging to them.

It wasn't easy. Every object carried the weight of a life lived. Every drawer held some thread of his history. But they did it together, sharing stories as they worked, laughing at the old tools he insisted on keeping, and wiping away tears when they found Christine's gardening journal, still marked with notations in her neat handwriting.

When the house was empty, Thomas stood in the doorway one last time. The air was still. The garden had gone quiet. He stepped outside and strolled to the blackberry bushes.

The leaves were beginning to turn, and a few berries—late bloomers—still clung to the vines. He picked one, held it between his fingers, and popped it into his mouth.

Sweet. Just like always.

Susan caught a flight back to California to ready the apartment for dad.

The drive back to California was long, but familiar. Both Thomas Jr and James took turns behind the wheel while watching the country unfold again through the windshield— fields and rivers and long stretches of open sky. Thomas dozed often, waking to James handing him a bottle of water or Thomas Jr. pointing out landmarks he'd forgotten.

And when they pulled into Susan's driveway on a sunny afternoon, she was waiting for them on the front steps with open arms and a warm smile that reminded him so much of her mother it made his heart ache.

"Welcome home, Daddy," she said.

She led him upstairs for lunch she had prepared for him

while Thomas Jr. and James unloaded the U-Haul. Susan came back down to announce that dad is taking a nap and helped unload.

When Thomas awoke, Susan took his hand and led him through a separate entrance that opened into the small apartment they had prepared for him. It was modest, but intentionally arranged—every detail considered. His favorite armchair sat in the corner by the window, a soft lamp casting a golden glow. The bookshelf held familiar titles, and above the fireplace hung a framed photo of Christine in the garden, smiling with her sunhat tilted to one side. At the foot of the bed lay the quilt she had sewn, the one he'd wrapped around himself during long Mississippi winters.

Thomas took a slow breath, letting it all settle in.

No, it wasn't Mississippi. The river didn't run outside the window, and the air didn't carry the same weight of memory. But it was warm. It was welcoming. A warmth that embraced and comforted overflowed within it.

This was home.

That evening, they ate dinner out on the patio—grilled chicken, corn pudding, and Susan's homemade cobbler. The grandkids ran barefoot across the grass, chasing each other in circles. Their laughter floated into the warm evening air, turning the night into something simple and beautiful, almost sacred.

Thomas sat back, his glass of sweet tea in hand, watching it all unfold.

There was still sorrow inside him, of course—Christine's absence, the ache of leaving the river behind, the creeping edge of time. But there was something else, too.

There was peace.

And gratitude.

And the quiet, powerful sense that, even near the end, life still had something beautiful to give.

Thomas's new life in California was quieter than he had expected—but it was exactly what he needed. The days moved at a gentle pace, free from stress or surprises. There was comfort in the routine: the smell of fresh coffee coming from Susan's kitchen each morning, the soft sounds of the neighborhood outside his window, and the quiet peace of being close to family again.

Susan often took him on short walks through nearby parks, guiding him arm-in-arm along tree-lined paths. They walked slowly, stopping to rest on benches and watch the world pass by—children flying kites, joggers nodding, couples walking dogs. On his better days, she would drive him to the local reservoir, where they'd sit together by the water's edge. Lines cast into the stillness.

Every 'now and then', they'd see an older black man fishing alone—quiet, patient, his eyes focused on the water. Thomas would feel something stir in his chest, a pang of longing, something deeper would settle in his heart. It was as if, for a moment, the years peeled away, and he was back on the riverbank in Mississippi with Jeremiah—two boys with big dreams and bare feet, talking about life and laughing at nothing at all.

Sometimes, Thomas would strike up a conversation. He'd share stories about his youth, about the Mississippi heat and the thick summer air, about catching catfish with his friend Jeremiah. He spoke of the laughter, the easy friendship, and the dreams they once nurtured together.

But only when the moment felt right—only when he sensed understanding—would he tell the rest.

As time went on, Thomas's health continued to decline. His body betrayed him more often. Cataracts clouded his vision, making it difficult for him to move around without help. His hands, once so sure and steady, trembled when he reached for a glass. Doctor appointments grew more frequent, and with each visit came a new pill, a new caution, a new piece of his independence slipping away.

Still, his spirit remained resilient.

The proper medicine came not from the pharmacy, but from the warmth that surrounded him—his family, his history, and the sense of legacy he had spent a lifetime building. His grandchildren visited often, filling the house with their noise and joy, peppering him with questions about the past. He would tell them stories of chasing fireflies, of building fence lines on the ranch, of dancing in the kitchen with Christine to old jazz records.

James, in particular, was a constant presence. He would sit with his father for hours—sometimes talking, sometimes just listening to the clock tick and the birds outside. The two men shared a bond now carved from hardship and healing. They would laugh together over old memories, fall into comfortable silence, and talk about the things most men leave unsaid.

One quiet afternoon in late fall, Thomas asked Susan to gather the family.

They all came—Susan, Thomas Jr., Ron, James, and even the older grandchildren. They sat with him in his small apartment; the air filled with a kind of reverent stillness. He sat in his favorite chair, a soft blanket over his legs, his voice a little hoarse but steady.

"There's something I want to talk about," he said, his gaze sweeping the room. "Something I've carried with me all my life."

They leaned in, not knowing what to expect.

He told them about Jeremiah—not just the name, but the boy. The friend. The laughter, the secrets, the dreams whispered along the riverbank. He painted a picture of youthful innocence, of a friendship so natural, so pure, that it felt like family. And then he told them what happened. The day they took Jeremiah. That hateful act that ended his friend's life and changed Thomas's forever.

His voice cracked as he spoke. He paused often, staring at a spot on the floor, lost in memory. His hands gripped the blanket as he described the rage, the helplessness, the guilt he had carried through the years—guilt for surviving, for not being able to stop it, for not speaking of it sooner.

Tears flowed openly—not just from Thomas, but from his children and grandchildren as well. They had known their father to be strong, principled, and emotional. But now, they saw the root of that strength. The pain that had shaped his silence. Grief had shaped his convictions. His legacy, shaped by love.

"I've always wanted to do right by him," Thomas whispered.

"That's why I've tried to be fair. To speak up when others were quiet. To treat people like they mattered. Because he did. And I couldn't save him... but I could live in a way that honored him."

There was nothing but silence for a long moment.

Then James stood, walked across the room, and placed a hand on his father's shoulder. "You did, Dad," he said. "You've honored him every day. And now we will too."

One by one, the others came forward—hugging him, thanking him, promising to carry that story, that truth, that memory forward. It was no longer a burden he bore alone. It was now a part of their family's story—a part of *them*.

And in that moment, Thomas felt something he hadn't expected: release. Not from grief. But from isolation. Jeremiah wasn't just his memory anymore. Jeremiah had spoken into the world. Seen. Known.

Remembered.

As Thomas's health continued to deteriorate, his family

stayed close, refusing to let him fade alone. His world had grown smaller in those last weeks—reduced to soft blankets, the quiet murmur of familiar voices, and the scent of lavender from the diffuser Susan kept by his bedside. But within that quiet, love surrounded him.

His children took turns sitting with him, holding his hand, reading from old journals or sharing stories from their childhood. The grandchildren would tiptoe in, unsure at first, then warm to him as he offered a smile or a whispered word of wisdom. Even as his body weakened, his spirit remained strong. He told James once, in the middle of the night, "This isn't the end, son. Just the part where we rest."

On December 13, 2009, in the early evening, as the light outside faded to soft indigo, Thomas passed away peacefully. He was not alone. Surrounded by the people he loved most— his children and grandchildren—he felt their hands gently holding his, their fingers brushing through his hair, their voices soft with gratitude and love as they whispered their goodbyes. It was a quiet comfort, a final embrace from the life he had built.

He took his final breath, his face calm, as if he were merely slipping into sleep.

His ultimate wish was simple and clear: to be returned to Mississippi. To the soil where he was born. To the land where his story began. It was where he had once lost everything and where, later in life, he had rediscovered a piece of himself. His children honored that request without hesitation.

On a gray and rainy day in January, his family gathered in the small cemetery just outside Quitman, Mississippi. The sky was low, the air cool and clean, and the trees stood bare, their branches reaching like arms toward the clouds. The rain in a gentle mist that fell on coats and umbrellas and the red Mississippi mud beneath their feet.

They stood in a quiet semicircle around the small plot, just a short distance from where Christine had been buried year before. The minister—a local man who had known Christine in her later years—spoke few words, choosing instead to let silence honor the man, whose ashes were being returned to the earth.

One by one, his children stepped forward. James carried the

urn, setting it decisively, into the small hollow in the ground. Susan knelt beside it and laid a single sprig of rosemary, her lips moving in silent prayer. Thomas Jr. placed a photo of the ranch they had once worked on together, and Ron tucked a folded handkerchief—one of their father's old ones—into the soil.

The mud was wet and rich and familiar, and it held him as if welcoming him home.

As the rain fell around them, mingling with tears and memories, they stood shoulder to shoulder, united not just in grief, but in gratitude. Their hearts were heavy, yes—but not broken. Their father had lived with purpose and grace. Through suffering, he still chose kindness. He had endured loss and still offered love. He had failed and tried again.

Returning to his origins, his journey had come full circle— the land where he'd learned to dream, fight, and forgive. Mississippi had given him joy and taken from him deeply. But in the end, it had also given him peace.

He could not save Jeremiah, the friend whose loss had haunted him all his life. But he had saved James. He had saved his family. He had given his children a life rooted in justice, in resilience, in the fierce, quiet power of dignity.

And now, even in death, he continued to give. His story—his truth—remained imprinted in the hearts of those who knew him. A father. A husband. A friend. A man who had wrestled with the world and come out on the other side not perfect, but whole.

Years later, his grandchildren would bring their own children to that same cemetery. They'd point to the small grave stone beneath the mulberry tree and say, "That's where your great-granddad is. He was a vigorous man. A kind man. He taught us how to live and how to stand up for what's right."

And so, Thomas's legacy endured—not in monuments or history books, but in the living fabric of his family. Amidst shared laughter over fishing poles. In stories told on porches. They hold hands during hard times. Remembering is a simple, sacred act.

Because in the end, Thomas Smith was never just a man

shaped by tragedy. He was a man who shaped *peace* from it. And that was the life he left behind.

The End

Conclusion

When I first set out to write this book, I thought I was preserving history. I thought I was documenting the life of my father—his trials, his strength, his quiet courage. But what I discovered as I put his story to paper was something much deeper: this book wasn't just about the past. It was about understanding the present. It was about reckoning with the weight we carry through generations—what we inherit, what we bury, and what we're conclusively brave enough to uncover.

My father, Thomas Franklin Smith, lived a life shaped by forces far larger than himself—poverty, racism, war, and injustice. But within those forces, he made choices. Quiet ones. Private ones. And ultimately, one that would define the rest of his life: the choice to stand up and protect his son, even if it meant risking everything.

He never intended to be a hero. Imperfect, he was. The burden of memory, guilt over his silence, and the shame of survival were his to carry. For years, he said nothing about what happened to Jeremiah. He rarely spoke of the pain of war. And he never asked for recognition for the moment he pulled the trigger in defense of his family. But in his silence lived a truth that demanded to be told.

This is that truth.

Throughout this journey, I've realized that justice doesn't always wear a badge or come with a verdict. Sometimes justice looks like a man driving cross-country to help his struggling son. A crow's call sometimes echoes through the Mississippi woods. At the edge of a dirt road, a single moment can change a man who once watched a friend die, making him refuse to let it happen again.

I didn't write this book to make anyone comfortable. I wrote it to tell the truth. And in that truth, I found healing. There are still people in this world who believe that silence is safer. That some stories are better left untold. That what happened "back then" should stay buried. But I've learned that silence is its own kind of wound. And sometimes, the only way to heal is to speak the unspeakable.

I hope readers see in my father what I saw: a man who struggled, who faltered, but who ultimately stood in the face of fear. A man who loved his family more than his own peace.

 A man who, even after a lifetime of carrying pain, found a way to use it—not as a weapon, but as a shield for those he loved.

This book is not just his story. It's my family's story. It's America's story. And if we're honest with ourselves, it's a story we all have a part in—whether as witnesses, participants, or descendants of choices made long ago. As I close these pages, I carry a deep gratitude for the man my father was. For the truth, he lived. For the silence, he broke. And for the strength he left behind in every one of us who bears his name.

May his story remind us that while injustice can shape a life, it does not have to define it.

And may we all have the courage, when the time comes, to stand.

Thomas Smith Jr.

Printed in Great Britain
by Amazon

63108329R00221